RODALE ORGANIC GARDENING BASICS

compost

RODALE

**From the Editors of
Rodale Organic Gardening
Magazine and Books**

RODALE
WE **INSPIRE** AND **ENABLE** PEOPLE TO IMPROVE
THEIR LIVES AND THE WORLD AROUND THEM

The information in this book has been carefully researched, and all efforts have been made to ensure accuracy. Rodale Inc. assumes no responsibility for any injuries suffered or for damages or losses incurred during the use of or as a result of following this information. It's important to study all directions carefully before taking any action based on the information and advice presented in this book. When using any commercial product, *always* read and follow label directions. Where trade names are used, no discrimination is intended and no endorsement by Rodale Inc. is implied.

Printed in the United States of America on acid-free ∞, recycled ♻ paper

We're always happy to hear from you. For questions or comments concerning the editorial content of this book, please write to

Rodale Book Readers' Service
33 East Minor Street
Emmaus, PA 18098

Look for other Rodale books wherever books are sold. Or call us at (800) 848-4735.

For more information about Rodale Organic Gardening magazine and books, visit us at

www.organicgardening.com

Editor: Vicki Mattern
Contributing Editor: Christine Bucks
Interior Book Designer: Nancy Smola Biltcliff
Cover Designer: Patricia Field
Interior Illustrator: Anthony Davis
Cover Photographer: Rob Cardillo
Photography Editor: Lyn Horst
Photography Assistant: Jackie L. Ney
Layout Designer: Dale Mack
Researchers: Diana Erney, Sarah Wolfgang Heffner
Copy Editors: Stacey Ann Follin, Amy Kovalski
Manufacturing Coordinator: Patrick T. Smith
Indexer: Nan Badgett
Editorial Assistance: Kerrie A. Cadden

RODALE ORGANIC GARDENING BOOKS
Executive Editor: Kathleen DeVanna Fish
Managing Editor: Fern Marshall Bradley
Executive Creative Director: Christin Gangi
Art Director: Patricia Field
Production Manager: Robert V. Anderson Jr.
Studio Manager: Leslie M. Keefe
Copy Manager: Nancy N. Bailey
Manufacturing Manager: Eileen Bauder

**Library of Congress
Cataloging-in-Publication Data**

Rodale organic gardening basics. Volume 8, Compost / from the editors of Rodale organic gardening magazine and books.
        p.   cm.
    Includes bibliographical references (p.   ) and index.
    ISBN 0-87596-856-2 (pbk. : alk. paper)
    1. Compost.   2. Organic gardening.   I. Title: Compost.   II. Rodale Books.   III. Organic gardening (Emmaus, Pa. : 1988)   IV. Title. V. Rodale organic gardening basics ; v 8.
S661 .R63-2001
631.8′75--dc21   00-011389

Distributed in the book trade by St. Martin's Press

2   4   6   8   10   9   7   5   3   paperback

contents

Food for the Soil

Imagine a diet of just plain water. Or how about a diet of water and powdered, tasteless nutritional powder? Yuck. It wouldn't leave you feeling satisfied, healthy, or full.

Well, a diet like that doesn't work for soil, either.

The only thing that truly feeds and satisfies the soil is more soil—in the form of compost. Compost is just recreating what nature does when people aren't around to harvest and clean up. When leaves fall in the forest or grasses die back in the prairie, they act as mulch; then, as they decompose, they become rich, dark, fluffy soil.

Rich, dark, fluffy soil is every gardener's dream. It's easy to plant in *and* plants thrive in it. Unfortunately, most of our gardens are not naturally endowed with rich, dark, fluffy soil.

That's why this book will show you how to make it yourself. Making compost is as easy as letting the leaves fall off the trees in the forest. And once your garden is rich and full of healthy soil, it will be able to deliver beautiful and delicious healthy food and flowers to you.

What goes around, comes around. You feed the soil with compost, and it will feed you with joy.

Once your garden is full of healthy soil, it will be able to deliver beautiful and delicious food and flowers to you.

Happy organic gardening!

Maria Rodale

Maria Rodale

Amending your soil with compost
is an excellent way to help grow
a luscious garden like this one.

chapter one

Go Organic: Composting Simplified

What is compost? Next time you walk through a wooded area, scoop up a handful of that dark, crumbly material on the forest floor: That's compost—nature's version. Compost simply is decomposed organic matter, but it's the best gift you can give your garden. And you can make it using materials you already have on hand.

6 REASONS WHY COMPOST IS GOOD FOR YOUR GARDEN

Making compost is probably the single most important thing you can do for your organic garden. The success of your garden depends on your soil, and the health of your soil depends on the compost you give it. Compost makes the soil loose and porous and increases the amount of water it can hold. Compost also slowly releases nutrients into the soil, giving plants a steady, balanced diet to keep them growing strong. There's even evidence that adding compost to your soil can protect plants from disease.

And making compost isn't difficult. With very little effort on your part, you can turn throw-away materials into the sweet-smelling, nutrient-rich, no-cost soil conditioner called "gardener's gold." At the same time, you're recycling kitchen scraps and yard wastes, instead of paying to have them hauled off to the local landfill. Not a bad deal!

Still not convinced that compost is worth making? Then turn the page to take a closer look at the six ways compost is indispensable for organic gardeners—starting with drought protection.

> With very little effort, you can turn throw-away materials into a no-cost soil conditioner.

1. Protects Plants from Drought

Soil that has been amended with compost holds more moisture. Compost encourages the formation of soil granules, which soak up water and hold it, like a sponge. (Humus—the end result of the composting process—is so absorbent that 100 pounds of it can hold 195 pounds of water!)

During drought, the tiny hairs on plant roots absorb all the water the plant needs from films that surround these granules.

So by adding compost to your soil, you won't need to water your plants as often. You could even vacation for a week or so without worrying that you'll come back to a baked garden.

2. Improves Soil Aeration

Aeration is extremely important to the health of your soil. Without air, soil tends to become alkaline. It also loses the organic matter and nitrogen that are essential to productivity. Humus content drops, too. And any humus that remains loses its potency.

Soil needs air to transform valuable minerals into forms that plants can use. Beneficial soil organisms—such as the mycorrhiza that help feed critical nutrients to plant roots—also require oxygen to thrive and reproduce.

In your garden, lack of aeration commonly shows up as crusting of the soil surface. Soil particles pack together, preventing water and air from entering. Seed germination could be poor because the sprouts have trouble pushing through the soil's hard surface.

The cure? Compost, of course. Adding compost to your soil will improve its structure and allow for optimum aeration at all times. Organic matter not only enables soil to hold more water through the formation of soil granules but also allows more spaces for air *between* the granules.

3. Stops Erosion

By improving soil structure and fertility, compost can prevent soil erosion.

Shortsighted agricultural practices already have led to the erosion and loss of much of America's topsoil. According to the USDA, as much as 6 billion tons of soil erodes away each year in the United States! Commercial agriculture—which can deplete organic matter and cause compaction—has been linked to more than two-thirds of all erosion. It's been estimated that for every pound of food eaten in the United States, water has eroded 22 pounds of agricultural soil.

In your own garden, you can prevent soil erosion by using compost. Soil that contains a lot of humus (finished compost) holds together better, and so can resist erosion by wind and water. Instead of running off the soil surface—taking your soil with it—water permeates the soil, moving easily through the spaces between granules.

If you add compost to your soil and keep it covered with mulch or garden plants, you should never have serious erosion problems like this farm field has suffered.

4. Slowly Releases Nutrients

Compost is a well-balanced source of most of the nutrients plants need. What's more, compost acts as a kind of nutrient storehouse, releasing nutrients in a form that's available gradually throughout the growing season. In spring, when plants are small, compost doles out nutrients slowly. Later, as the soil warms up

COLLOIDS: UP CLOSE AND PERSONAL

HUMUS—THE END product of compost—holds nutrients in soil and makes them easily available to plants. But how, you might wonder, do the nutrients get from the soil to the plants? Colloidal (very tiny) humus particles have a negative charge, so they attract positive elements like potassium, sodium, calcium, magnesium, iron, and copper. When a tiny rootlet comes into contact with humus, it trades hydrogen ions for these mineral (nutrient) ions.

In soils that are low in colloids (humus), minerals easily leach out in rain. That's why plants growing in low-humus soils commonly grow very quickly after a rain—they're absorbing the minerals that have dissolved in the rainwater. When drought sets in, though, plant growth comes to a halt. In contrast, humus-rich organic soils encourage steady growth, regardless of rainfall. Plants draw on the minerals held on the colloids that are plentiful in humusy soil.

and plant growth accelerates, nutrients are released at a faster rate. That's because the soil microorganisms that release the nutrients from compost work harder as the temperature rises.

As compost breaks down into humus, it improves the soil's ability to store nutrients. So if you amend your soil regularly with compost, plant nutrients can build up over time to the point that the soil needs little fertilizer of any kind for several years. (No chemical fertilizers can make that claim.) And that saves you both time and money.

Depending on what ingredients went into the compost, a given batch can be high or low in certain elements. The greater the variety of materials you use to make your compost, the greater the variety of nutrients it will contain—that includes both the major plant nutrients (nitrogen, phosphorus, and potassium) and the micronutrients (such as iron, manganese, and boron).

Plants need only very small amounts of micronutrients, but these minor elements are essential to plant growth and reproduction (which is why it's important to vary what you put in your pile). Many soils don't have enough iron, manganese, boron, zinc, cobalt, copper, molybdenum, or iodine for good plant health— a problem that compost can easily remedy. (*Note:* Some soils contain too *much* of one or more of these micronutrients, which can harm plants. To determine specific nutrient levels in your soil, have a reputable soil lab test your soil. Whether the soil has too little or too much of a certain element, adding compost usually corrects the problem.) You can call your local cooperative extension office to find the lab nearest you.

5. Prevents Disease

Compost has seemingly miraculous powers to prevent and control plant disease. Just an inch of compost spread over the soil's surface will fight plant diseases better than any chemical fungicide.

Many scientific studies document compost's disease-controlling benefits. Here are some examples of what it can do for your garden.

- Florida studies have shown that compost can protect pepper plants from phytophthora root rot; dramatically reduce damping-off (a disease that causes seedlings to keel over and die) and gummy stem blight in squash plants; reduce rhizoctonia (a fungal disease) by 80 percent in black-eyed peas; reduce early blight and root-knot nematode damage; and virtually eliminate macrophomina (another nasty fungal disease) from green beans.

A BETTER BUFFER

BEFORE YOU GET out that bag of limestone or sulfur to correct an apparent pH imbalance, first try a liberal application of compost. You could find that compost alone solves the problem.

By adding humus to the soil, compost helps plants withstand soil pH levels that are either too low (such as in the Upper Midwest and Northeast) or too high (such as in the Southwest). Humus acts as a buffer in the soil, and when soil has an abundant supply of it, growing garden crops become less dependent on specific soil pH levels.

Many plants that are said to prefer acidic or alkaline soil actually just need nutrients that becomes unavailable when the pH isn't within a desired range. Compost makes those nutrients more available and helps keep extreme pH from making the valuable nutrients insoluble.

• California researchers used compost to eliminate brown rot on peaches (a fungal disease that causes fruit to turn brown and soft). Fruit from the compost-treated orchard had no brown rot, while 24 percent of the fruit from a neighboring orchard (treated with chemical fungicides) did have it.

• A New York country club uses compost to combat turf diseases and was able to cut its fungicide use 97 percent after just 3 years.

• Compost tea—the liquid produced by steeping compost in water—has been found to prevent mildew on plants.

Paradoxically, leaving *uncomposted* plant residues on your garden at the end of the season can actually cause problems because they provide a haven for overwintering pests and diseases. That's all the more reason to clean up your garden and turn those wastes into disease-preventing gardener's gold.

6. Recycles Wastes

When you make compost, you recycle wastes—grass clippings, leaves, spent garden plants, and kitchen scraps—that otherwise would end up being dumped in the landfill or burned. Composting saves not only landfill space but also the precious nutrients contained in the organic matter. In fact, composting is the only form of waste disposal that conserves these nutrients so they can, eventually, be returned to the soil. The entire ecosystem benefits.

Composting also helps the environment by reducing the use of chemical fertilizers. Unlike compost, chemical fertilizers are made from nonrenewable resources. Manufacturing ammonia fertilizers, for instance, requires the use of natural gas: About 2 percent of the natural gas consumed in the United States goes to the making of nitrogen fertilizers. Natural gas supplies are

quick tip

Wood chip mulches are a great weed barrier—and they last a long time, so you don't have to replace them often. But wood chips can tie up soil nitrogen. So what's a gardener to do?

Compost solves the problem. It gives soil microbes a rich source of nutrients as they work on digesting the wood chips, so the microbes don't have to raid all the nitrogen that's present in your soil while they do their work. Just spread a layer of compost on the soil you want to mulch before you put down those nitrogen-stealing wood chips. (In a landscape planting, this gives you and your plants the advantages of both mulch and compost.)

finite, and shortages are bound to occur in the future.

Instead of buying fertilizers that use up natural resources, pollute water, deteriorate soil structure, and kill beneficial microorganisms, you can make compost. At the same time, you'll be keeping organic wastes out of the landfill. If you can't manage all of your organic wastes in a home compost pile, take them to the closest municipal composting center—but don't put them out with the trash!

Turn today's news into tomorrow's compost by adding shredded black-and-white newspaper to your pile.

10 THINGS YOU CAN STOP DOING NOW

If you've never tried composting before, check out this list of things you can stop doing when you start composting:

1. STOP Using Synthetic Fertilizers!

Feeding your plants with synthetic (also called "chemical") fertilizers gives you short-term gains in growth at the expense of long-term soil health. Because they're highly soluble, synthetic fertilizers tend to wash through the soil quickly. If plants don't use them, they end up as pollutants in groundwater, rivers, and lakes. They're also harmful to earthworms and other soil organisms that work hard at turning organic matter into humus and nutrients for your plants.

Instead, feed your plants with compost you've made yourself. You'll save money and make your soil and plants happy at the same time.

quick tip

Save vegetable peelings, eggshells, coffee grounds, tea bags, and apple cores for the compost pile (just keep a plastic bucket with a lid on the kitchen counter for collecting them). If you have big kitchen leftovers—such as broccoli stalks, corncobs, or uncooked pumpkin rinds—slice or chop them up before you add them to your compost (unless you want to see a really scary jack-o-lantern smiling up at you come spring). Citrus peels need to be cut into especially small pieces—1-inch strips—or they won't break down.

2. STOP Throwing Kitchen Scraps in the Garbage!

When you toss out kitchen scraps—such as eggshells, potato peels, coffee grounds, and apple cores—you're throwing away potential nutrients for your garden. Instead, start a compost pile, add your kitchen scraps to it, and watch them turn into a rich organic amendment for your garden soil.

3. STOP Spraying Your Plants with Pesticides!

Chemical pesticides do much more than kill pests: They also kill beneficial insects and microorganisms living in your soil. And the pesticide residues left on plants can make you and your family very sick. But after you begin to use compost on your garden, you'll find that you won't even need pesticides. Just one example: Researchers at Ohio State University found that corn grown in compost-amended soil had 18 times fewer corn borer eggs than corn grown in chemically fertilized soil! Compost improves your soil's health, which in turn increases plants' resistance to pest insects.

4. STOP Watering So Often!

When you start adding compost to your garden soil, you won't need to water your plants as often. Compost acts as a sponge, storing water and then releasing it to plant roots as needed.

5. STOP Using So Much Bagged Mulch!

Covering your soil with a layer of mulch is a great way to conserve soil moisture, moderate soil temperatures, block weeds, and prevent soil erosion. But buying tons of bagged mulch to cover all of your garden beds can become expensive.

The good news is that you won't need to buy so much mulch (maybe you won't need to buy any!) if you use compost as mulch. Compost makes an ideal organic mulch for all of your garden beds. It offers all of the usual benefits of mulch—and more. Just an inch of compost, spread on the soil's surface as mulch, will protect plants from disease better than any chemical fungicide.

6. STOP **Using Herbicides on Your Lawn!**

Herbicides can leave poisonous residues on your lawn that can hurt kids and pets. They also kill beneficial soil microorganisms and can pollute groundwater. Therefore, you don't want to put herbicide-treated grass clippings into your compost pile or on your garden beds as mulch.

But when you start making compost, you won't have any need for those nasty herbicides anyway. Just spread a ¼-inch layer of compost over your lawn at least once a season. Your grass will become so lush and healthy that weeds won't be able to compete.

7. STOP **Throwing Away Grass Clippings and Leaves!**

Instead of bagging these common yard wastes and paying to have them hauled away, mix them together to make quick-cooking compost. Grass clippings and leaves provide nitrogen-rich and carbon-rich materials—both of which are needed to make great compost. Carbon-rich stuff (also known as "dry browns") includes leaves, hay, and straw. Nitrogen-rich goodies (also called "wet greens") include grass clippings, garden plant wastes, and weeds.

Grass clippings are an excellent source of nitrogen, which is a "must have" ingredient for any compost pile.

Help protect peat bogs (and save money, too) by using compost instead of peat as a soil amendment.

8. STOP Buying Peat!

Although peat moss is a popular soil amendment and covering, peat is a limited resource. And as more countries move to protect their native bogs, peat moss is becoming more expensive. Many gardeners are discovering that peat moss isn't such a great mulch or soil amendment anyway.

When used as mulch, peat moss can crust over and prevent moisture from penetrating your soil. And as a soil amendment, peat not only is hard to wet and rewet but also has limited nutrient value. So save your money, and use compost instead. Finished compost adds humus, retains moisture, and aerates and fertilizes your soil.

9. STOP Using So Much Potting Soil!

Bagged potting soils vary in quality and cost. Why take a chance? Well-aged compost (at least 6 months old) makes an excellent, free potting soil and seed-starting medium.

10. STOP Tilling So Much!

If your garden soil is packed together and has a crust on top, you might have a tendency to get out there and till, till, till, to try to loosen things up. But tilling your soil too much can actually make the matter worse. When you add lots of compost to your soil, though, all that humus helps with aeration, thereby increasing the health of your soil.

FOLLOW THE CYCLE

Whether decomposition takes place on the forest floor or in your compost pile, the systems at work are the same, and humus is always the result.

The Carbon Cycle

In nature's carbon cycle, green plants use carbon dioxide, air, water, and sunlight to make sugars and other carbon-containing compounds that animals use as food. The carbon compounds in plant and animal wastes then provide food for decomposers in the compost pile. Finished compost contains beneficial microorganisms and nutrients used by a new generation of growing plants, continuing the cycle.

The Nitrogen Cycle

Composting also plays a part in nature's "nitrogen cycle." Plants need nitrogen to grow. But plants can't easily use the nitrogen in the atmosphere ("nitrogen-fixing" plants rely on symbiotic bacteria), so their growth is limited to the amount of nitrogen they can get from the soil. Compost helps make more nitrogen available to plants. In the compost pile, plant and animal wastes are exposed to nitrogen-fixing microorganisms and decomposers. As these organic materials break down, their nitrogen becomes available in forms that growing plants can use.

Plants, animals, and microscopic decomposers all play an integral role in nature's carbon cycle.

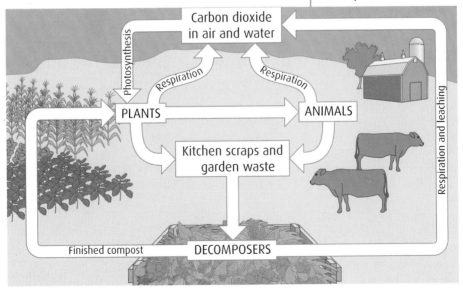

Making compost is a lot easier— and a lot more fun—when you have the right tools.

chapter two

Tools & Supplies

Truth is, you can make compost without any tools or equipment. But if you want to cook up big batches of "gardener's gold," compost bins, tumblers, frames, and other gadgets can help you do the job quickly and easily.

GOOD INVESTMENTS

Compost happens. Just pile up your grass clippings, fallen leaves, garden wastes, and kitchen scraps and the materials eventually will decompose into rich, black humus.

Although equipment isn't essential for making good compost, it can help you manage your composting operation. Here are some reasons why you might want to invest in a compost bin, frame, tumbler, or other equipment.

Appearance matters. If you have a small yard and have to make compost in full view of your neighbors, you (and your neighbors) may be happier if your compost is under cover.

Bins boost production. Compost bins can help you organize your composting so that you can be more productive. For example, with a three-bin system, you can pile slowly decomposing yard wastes in one bin, mix kitchen scraps and finely chopped materials for fast composting in another bin, and keep finished compost in the third bin. Or, use one bin for finished compost, and turn your compost-in-progress from one of the remaining bins into the other.

Get finished compost faster. By turning and aerating your pile—using a tumbler, pitchfork, and other kinds of equipment—you can speed the process and turn garbage into gold in almost no time at all.

7 Helpful Composting Tools

- **Compost bin or tumbler**
- **Pitchfork**
- **Wheelbarrow**
- **Screen**
- **Thermometer**
- **Aerator**
- **Hose**

BUILD-IT-YOURSELF BINS

Whatever your composting style, there's bound to be a bin, frame, or tumbler that'll meet your needs. If you're handy, you can build your own compost bin in almost no time at all. You can use almost any durable material, including wire, wood, slats, and cinder blocks. Here are a few ideas.

Wire Cage

Easy does it: Start with a 10-foot length of 48-inch 12½- or 14-gauge welded steel wire fencing. Clip or wire together the ends to form a cylindrical compost bin 4 feet high and slightly more than 3 feet across. Pile your leaves, clippings, and other organic materials inside. (Use grass clippings sparingly, in layers no more than 1 inch thick, to avoid matting.) When the bin is half full, drive a stake into the center of the pile. Water will run down the stake, helping to keep the pile moist.

To turn the pile, simply unfasten the bin's ends, pull the fencing away from the materials, and set the bin back up next to the heap. Then, refill the empty bin, turning the materials from the top of the original pile to the bottom of the new pile and from the outside to the inside.

When your wire bin is half-full, drive a stake into the middle of the pile. That way, water will run down the stake to help keep the pile moist.

Wood and Wire Bin

For a bit more structure, make a wood and wire bin, using untreated 2 × 4 lumber and ½-inch mesh hardware cloth or poultry netting. (*Never use pressure-treated wood*—toxic copper and arsenic will leach into your compost and eventually contaminate your garden soil; cedar is a good choice because it resists rotting.) Use the lumber to make four 3 × 3-foot or 4 × 4-foot identical open frames. Staple the hardware cloth to one side of each frame. Next, nail three of the panels together to form a back and two sides. Use the remaining panel to make a convenient door, by hinging the edges at one corner and placing the hooks and eyes on the opposite corner. To turn the compost ingredients, just open the hooks for easy access.

A variation of this is the wire and tomato stake bin. Make a 4 × 4-foot square by driving 4-foot-long tomato stakes into the ground at 1-foot intervals. Surround the stakes with the hardware cloth or wire netting, then loop baling wire around the whole thing to secure the netting.

The wire in a wood-and-wire bin will help keep pesky rodents out of the pile. Removable slats in the movable slat bin make for easy access to your compost.

Set up these bins close to where you need to use compost. When you've used up the compost, move the bin to another location in need of compost, and begin a new pile.

Movable Slat Bin

Perhaps the classic compost bin is the movable slat bin (sometimes called the New Zealand box). Because slat bins are constructed entirely of wood, they hold up better than wire bins.

The sides of these bins consist of movable slats that fit inside tracks. Spacers between the slats allow air to reach the compost materials, speeding the breakdown

process. The slats make access easy: When you need to work with the composting materials, you just remove as many of the slats as necessary.

Many movable slat bins have three compartments for storing compost in various stages: freshly collected materials, partially decomposed materials, and finished compost. Having multiple bins allows you to produce a continuous supply of compost for all your garden needs.

The ideal size bin for making quick compost should hold 27 cubic feet of organic material. To keep out animals like racoons and rodents, attach hinged lids to the top of each bin. Bins like these can be made with or without a floor. Your compost will break down faster, however, without a floor—just pile the materials directly on the ground.

(Remember, use cedar or another rot-resistant wood to make a wooden bin, instead of using pressure-treated wood.)

Cinder Block Bin

If you're looking for durability in a compost bin, cinder blocks are the way to go.

If durability is your chief concern, construct a permanent bin from cinder blocks (or brick) and mortar. For a bit more mobility out of the bin, use just the blocks without the mortar.

Stack the blocks three or four high to form walls. You can leave one side open to form a U-shaped bin or enclose the bin on all four sides. If you enclose all four sides, lay the blocks apart—with spaces of 1 inch or more between them—to improve air circulation. Add one or more interior walls to create multiple bins. To turn the pile,

simply remove the blocks from one side and fork the materials from one bin to another.

Cover the structure with a wooden lid or plastic tarp to keep rain out. If you make a concrete floor for your bin, make sure you slant it slightly to allow drainage. (Collect the resulting "compost tea" in a bucket and use it to feed houseplants!)

For winter protection, consider recessing the bin into a slope that has good southern exposure. A 5 × 10-foot cinder block bin can hold 2 to 3 tons of compost.

Miscellaneous Bins

Compost bins come in all shapes, sizes, and materials. Feel free to use whatever you have on hand. Resourceful gardeners have been known to use such things as pallets, picket or snow fencing, and straw bales to make quality compost bins.

Pallets. Recycled hardwood pallets provide a quick, easy—and commonly free—compost bin. Just stand the pallets on end in a square, pound in fence posts to hold the corners together, and use heavy-gauge wire to fasten the pallets to the posts.

Fencing. Fencing is sturdy and allows plenty of air to circulate inside the bin. Use steel or wooden posts for the bin's corners. Attach snow, lattice, or picket fencing for the sides.

Straw bales. You can make an all-organic compost bin by using straw bales—stacked two high—for the sides. Move away a bale or two to turn and access the compost. Over time, some of the straw itself will decompose, adding more carbon to your pile.

Straw bale bins do double duty. Over time, some of the straw will decompose, adding more carbon to your pile.

READY-MADE COMPOSTERS

Ready-made composters may cost you more than the materials for making your own bin. But commercial composters can be quite attractive and durable. They also save you the time and effort you'd spend making your own. There are two basic types—bins and tumblers—with many variations of each.

A dark-colored plastic commercial bin is a good choice if you live where the climate's cold because the bin will catch and hold the sun's heat.

Commercial Bins

Many of these composters are made of recycled plastic, which won't warp or discolor like wood. Bins made of dark-colored plastic catch and hold the sun's heat, making them good choices for those who live in frigid climates.

Some of these bins retain moisture, too. Their sides and top cover are slanted to catch just enough rain to maintain moisture levels without drenching the compost. And while you do have to turn the compost the old-fashioned way—using a pitchfork—you don't have to uncover the composter to do so. You just insert your fork through a mixing slot near the top, loosen and turn the material, then insert the fork into one of the lower slots to mix the material on the bottom. Removable doors on the sides allow you to scoop out the finished compost. With a pliers, you can assemble the unit in about half an hour.

You can even buy an inexpensive—and "compostable"—cardboard container that will hold your compost for about a year before it's ready to become one with its contents. At that point, you can just toss it into another cardboard bin and start again!

Compost Tumblers

Tumbler or drum composters are plastic or metal containers that are usually mounted on elevated frames. Some models have gear-driven turning mechanisms; others spin on ball bearings. Another type resembles a large metal or plastic ball. To turn the contents, you just roll the ball on the ground.

Because tumblers make it easy to turn materials, they can produce compost quickly. They have at least one drawback, however. Their capacity usually isn't very large. When you've filled the tumbler to a certain level, you must stop adding fresh materials until the process has finished. During those 2 to 3 weeks, you'll need to stockpile your materials in another container or area. And because the contents rest on plastic rather than on the ground, you might want to add a few shovelfuls of soil or finished compost whenever you fill the bin. Otherwise, earthworms won't be able to get in to help the decomposition process.

If you're looking for a bin that makes turning materials easy, choose a compost tumbler.

Deciding What to Buy

Don't choose a commercial composter based on its cost alone. Consider these factors, too:

Portability. Some models, especially the tumblers, are too large or heavy to move easily. Make sure you have a good site for such a bin before you buy it. Portable bins (like the ball type) allow you to make compost at several sites around the garden; they're especially good for gardeners who don't have a wheelbarrow or who garden over a large area.

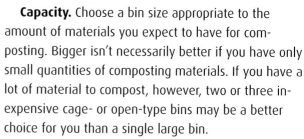

quick tip

If you've had raccoons, opossums, or some other scavenging animal tearing at your pile in the past, you'll find it difficult to break them of the habit. Your best bet is to buy a completely enclosed bin or tumbler to keep garbage hounds away. (And remember not to add meat scraps or fat to your pile!)

Capacity. Choose a bin size appropriate to the amount of materials you expect to have for composting. Bigger isn't necessarily better if you have only small quantities of composting materials. If you have a lot of material to compost, however, two or three inexpensive cage- or open-type bins may be a better choice for you than a single large bin.

Ease of assembly. Some of the more complicated bins are sold unassembled and have dozens of pieces to screw and bolt together. If possible, read the assembly instructions before you buy.

Ease of use. If the bin has a loading door or lid, you should be able to lift or open and close it easily. The opening should be wide enough to accommodate bulky material. When considering a drum-type composter, check to see that there's enough room beneath the drum to park a wheelbarrow for unloading the finished compost.

OTHER COMPOSTING TOOLS

Besides the items in the following list, there are at least a few other tools that can help you make compost. For instance, you'll probably want a small bucket with a lid (for collecting and carrying kitchen scraps) and a pair of good-quality gloves. Many gardeners also find a chipper/shredder useful for chopping leaves and garden wastes into smaller pieces before adding them to the pile: The smaller the pieces, the faster they'll decompose.

Forks

Use a pitchfork—which has three long, slightly rounded tines—to add materials to the pile, to turn the pile, and to transfer the finished compost to your wheelbarrow and beds. Use a straw fork (with five or six long rounded tines) for scattering light composting material.

Straw fork

Wheelbarrow

Of course you'll need a wheelbarrow (or garden cart) to transport your grass clippings, leaves, and garden wastes to the compost pile and to carry your finished compost to your garden. Wheelbarrows also are handy to work over when screening compost or potting up houseplants.

You'll find wheelbarrows easier to maneuver than heavy-duty garden carts because they have one wheel instead of two. And with plastic models, maintenance is minimal—they have no metal parts to rust.

Wheelbarrow

Screen

A screen is useful for separating the finer particles of finished compost from larger, less-decayed chunks. Fine, screened compost is ideal for covering seedbeds. If it's aged (6 months or more), you can even use it in potting mixes. Throw the larger stuff back into the pile for further microbial breakdown, or—if the pieces aren't too big—use it as mulch or sidedressing for plants that are already established.

You can either buy a compost screen or make your own by stapling hardware cloth or fine-gauge chicken wire to a simple wood frame.

Screen

Thermometer

If you want to make compost quickly (in as little as 2 to 3 weeks), you'll need a compost thermometer to monitor the temperature of your pile. The hotter the temperature, the faster the decomposition. Another advantage of "hot compost" is that it kills weed seeds and disease organisms.

Use the thermometer to check the temperature every 3 to 5 days. When the temperature drops below

Compost thermometer

120°F, aerate the pile (by turning or using a commercial aerator) to get it cooking again.

You'll find compost thermometers at your garden center and in garden-supply catalogs. They're also useful for checking soil temperature.

Aerator

The more air you get into your pile, the faster it'll break down. There may be other benefits, too: Some research indicates that aerating your pile regularly could even boost its nitrogen content and disease-fighting abilities.

Turning your pile with a fork a couple of times a week is one way to get air into it. Another is to use a tool designed specifically for this purpose. Commercially sold compost aerators come in several styles. All have a long shaft that you use to twist, turn, or bore holes into the center of the pile. Most are hand-powered, but at least one model is powered by a standard power drill.

A low-effort alternative is the compost "chimney." A compost chimney is simply a piece of PVC pipe about 4 feet in length—slightly longer than the height of your pile—with holes drilled in it. You just stick the pipe upright in the center of the pile to allow air to flow through the decaying materials.

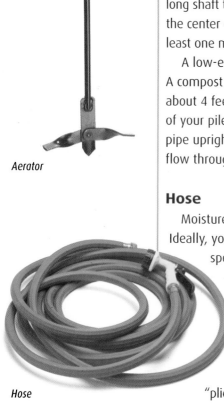

Aerator

Hose

Moisture is essential to the composting process. Ideally, your pile should feel as moist as a damp sponge (no wetter!). When the materials begin to dry out—causing the process to slow—you'll need to remoisten the layers with a hose.

If you're buying a new hose, look for a durable rubber hose with solid brass couplings. Also, keep in mind that the more "plies" it has, the better it will hold up.

Hose

MATERIALS FOR COMPOSTING

The ingredients for composting are all around you. Most gardeners have all they need right at home: grass clippings, leaves, kitchen scraps, weeds, and garden debris—almost anything that once lived is compostable!

Let's take a closer survey of organic materials suitable for composting, starting in your kitchen.

Kitchen Scraps

Kitchen scraps are relatively high in nitrogen. They also contain calcium, phosphorus, potassium, and micronutrients. Eggshells, coffee grounds, and vegetable and fruit peelings all can be converted to compost. Coffee grounds are especially good ingredients: Earthworms seem to love them.

Collect your kitchen scraps in a covered

Adding crushed eggshells to a compost pile can supply some extra calcium.

plastic or stainless steel container. Recycled plastic buckets with tight-fitting lids, such as those used for laundry detergent or wallboard compound, make excellent containers for storing up to a week's worth of goodies. (To keep family and guests happy, don't let your compostables accumulate indoors much longer than a week.) Add a layer of peat moss or sawdust to the bottom of the bucket to help absorb moisture and odors.

Note: Don't put meat scraps, grease, dairy products, or fat in your collection—they'll attract unwanted critters to your pile.

COLLECTING MATERIALS for your compost begins, of course, at home. *Anything* organic can be composted. That includes newspapers, tea bags, and clippings from your children's haircuts, as well as the usual yard and garden debris. Neighbors who collect their grass clippings may be happy to have you take them off their hands. The week after Halloween can be particularly bountiful, yielding cornstalks, straw bales, and the leaves that stuff those easy-to-spot bright orange, pumpkin-face bags.

From there, the possibilities are endless. For starters, look to area businesses. Orchards, factories, mills, stables, barbers, supermarkets, and restaurants all can be fertile gathering grounds. Useful materials you might find could include:

- Stable litter
- Orchard litter
- Peanut shells
- Vegetable trimmings
- Pet hair

Hair, Newspaper, and Other Goodies

Have pets? Their hair can go into the pile, too. And so, for that matter, can yours. Don't be shy: Collect your "trimmings" from your stylist or barber. Hair is an excellent source of nitrogen for the compost pile. Vacuum cleaner accumulations and dryer lint are fine for composting, too. And don't forget paper—shred up newspaper and computer paper and add them to the heap. They'll break down fast when mixed with high-nitrogen materials.

Sawdust

If there's a woodworker in the house, you probably have some sawdust on hand to add to the mix. It acts as a bulking agent, allowing air to penetrate the pile. (Don't use the very fine material left from sanding, however—it can pack down and slow the composting process.) Like paper, sawdust is high in carbon and low in nitrogen, so use it sparingly.

Grass Clippings and Garden Debris

Outdoors you'll find a wealth of organic materials at your disposal. Green materials—such as grass clippings, weeds, and garden debris—contain lots of nitrogen to speed the decay process. (For more on nitrogen and carbon content in organic materials, see Chapter 4.)

You can either rake your grass clippings or bag them as you mow. (Don't gather all of them, though—leave some on your lawn. As they break down, they add valuable nitrogen and organic matter to the soil, stimulating healthy new grass growth.) To avoid bending and picking up the clippings, simply rake the clippings onto a tarp, then drag them to your pile. Add them in thin layers to the pile, then mix them in thoroughly. Otherwise, they'll mat down and become slimy because of their high water content.

Note: Don't put herbicide-treated grass clippings in your compost pile. If you want to use your neighbor's clippings, first ask whether they've sprayed their lawn with any herbicides.

To collect garden wastes, carry a plastic bucket with you as you work. Toss in your prunings, weeds, and other debris. When you finish, just empty the contents onto your pile.

Leaves

Leaves are very valuable for composting. Trees have extensive root systems, allowing them to draw nutrients from deep in the soil. Much of this mineral bounty is passed into the leaves, making them a superior compost addition. Pound for pound, the leaves of most trees contain twice the mineral content of manure. Leaves also have plenty of fiber, which helps improve the aeration and crumb structure of soil.

Leaves don't contain much nitrogen, though. Like sawdust, newspaper, and straw, leaves are considered brown materials because they contain higher levels of carbon and break down more slowly than green materials, such as grass clippings.

Help fallen leaves break down faster by shredding them before adding them to your compost pile.

So you'll need to mix your leaves with a high-nitrogen green material to speed the decay process. (Combining only leaves and grass clippings will give you beautiful compost in about a month if you turn the pile weekly.)

Note that grinding or shredding leaves before you add them to the pile also will speed their breakdown. If you don't have a chipper/shredder, just run your lawn mower over the fallen leaves.

Keep in mind that you'll need more leaves and other browns to make compost. To accumulate enough leaves, you might need to stockpile them. After raking leaves in fall, many gardeners store them in plastic trash bags or in large cylinders made from chicken wire or snow fencing until spring, when more green materials become available for composting.

You also can make pure leaf compost (also called "leaf mold"). Just moisten those piled leaves and wait for them to break down on their own. In about a year, they will decompose into a black, powdery substance, similar to what you see on the forest floor. Leaf mold makes a great mulch because it releases nutrients slowly and retains an amazing amount of moisture.

REGIONAL RICHES

If you can't find enough organic materials at home to meet all of your composting needs, don't despair. Most regions have a wealth of organic riches—including apple pomace, mushroom soil, and crab shells—absolutely free for the taking. By locating these wastes and putting them to work in your garden, you can improve your soil and help the environment by reducing the amount of "fill" that goes into landfills.

Here's just a sample of the compost ingredients available in bulk, region by region.

Northeast

The Northeast is rich in compostable ingredients, such as fish scraps, sawdust, and apple pomace, to name a few.

Fish scraps. Fish is particularly abundant along the eastern coast of Canada and Maine, where more than 36,000 tons of fish waste is produced each year! Depending on the type of fish, the nitrogen and phosphorus levels can be as high as 8 percent and potassium can reach 2 percent.

But avoid using straight fish scraps on your garden: The "aroma" might not agree with you or your neighbors. Instead, mix the scraps with such compost ingredients as wood waste (including sawdust, wood chips, and bark), which is also locally abundant. University researchers suggest mixing 2½ parts sawdust with 1 part fish waste, by weight, for starters.

Apple pomace. You might also want to visit local canneries, cider mills, and orchards. Apple cider mills and juice processors produce tons of apple

Apple pomace, the residue left after cider is made, is a compost ingredient that's readily available in the Northeast.

pomace, the residue left after cider is made. Apple pomace is low in nitrogen, very wet, and acidic, but if you mix it with leaves and poultry manure, you'll get a good, nutritionally balanced compost. Adding a bit of wood ash will help neutralize the acidity.

Southeast

Southeastern compost riches include poultry litter, crab and crawfish wastes, and peanut shells.

Poultry litter. Each year, Alabama alone produces 1.7 million tons of poultry litter—manure mixed with the absorbent sawdust or peanut hulls that cover the chicken house floor. The best time to visit your local poultry farmer to pick up some of that litter is winter, right after farmers have finished cleaning out their broiler houses. After you've brought the litter home, let it compost until spring so it'll be nice and cool by the time you spread it on your garden.

Fish wastes. Like all regions with coastal areas, the Southeast also has its share of fish wastes. Besides pro-

If you live in the Southeast, you should be able to find plenty of peanut shells (a good source of nitrogen) for your compost pile.

viding plenty of plant-growth promoting nitrogen, the shells of crabs, shrimp, and crawfish also contain *chitin*—a naturally occurring substance that controls root-knot nematodes, a serious problem in southern gardens!

Lousiana's bayous are teeming with crawfish, and their carcasses are wonderfully compostable. For a good supply of shells, check with anyone who's having a "crawfish boil." Usually, there are plenty of heads and shells around after the seafood celebration is over. Some southern gardeners layer the shells with leaves to make a very rich, fast-cooking compost.

Denser lobster and crab shells also break down completely, if you turn the pile regularly. They'll break down even faster if you grind them up before adding them to the pile. Clam shells, also abundant in the Southeast, *must* be ground up before you compost them.

Peanut shells. Peanut shells and hulls and sugar cane "bagasse" (leftover after sugar cane is processed) are plentiful as well. Peanut shells are a good source of nitrogen (3.6 percent) for the compost pile. Sugar cane, on the other hand, is fibrous and slow to break down. Compost it with something high in nitrogen, such as peanut or shellfish waste. Some sugar cane processors will load up your truck with aged bagasse mixed with a little soil for about $5.

Midwest

The heartland might not have as much fish waste as coastal areas, but it does have plenty of slaughter-house waste and whey for your compost pile.

Slaughterhouse waste. This resource—which contains partially decomposed animal feed—is high in nitrogen and digestive enzymes, making it quick to decompose. Many experienced gardeners consider it one of the very best compost ingredients.

Whey. This liquid separates from curds during the cheese-making process and is potassium rich (15 percent). And there's plenty of whey to go around. According to one estimate, cheese factories in the United States produce more than 2 million tons of whey each year, with as much as half of it going to waste. (*Note:* You can even apply whey directly to your soil, but be careful not to apply more than 1 gallon per square foot per year. More than that could add too much sodium to your soil.)

Southwest

In this area of the country, you'll find cotton gin trash and vegetable wastes available for home compost piles.

Cotton gin trash. This is the noncloth- and nonoil-making part of cotton—and it's plentiful in the South, especially in Texas. Cotton burrs in particular are a good source of carbon for the compost pile. And you may even be able to get them from organic cotton farms: Texas has several thousand acres of organic cotton fields.

Vegetable waste. For vegetable wastes, don't forget the salsa factories. You may find, as other Southwesterners have, that local sauce factories will gladly deliver their leftover onions and peppers right to your home (it saves them money on waste removal fees).

THE BENEFITS OF CHOCOLATE

IF YOU'RE FORTUNATE enough to live near a chocolate factory, your garden could be in for a real treat! Cocoa bean shells—the residues from chocolate factories—are rich in nutrients and can be used in the compost pile or as an attractive mulch.

Cocoa shell dust is 1 percent nitrogen, 1.5 percent phosphorus, and 1.7 percent potassium. Untreated raw shells contain even more nutrients.

Sometimes cocoa shells are treated to extract the oil and theobromine, a naturally occurring substance in chocolate. Because lime is used in the extraction process, the resulting shells tend to have an alkaline pH. You can use these alkaline cocoa shells to help balance acidic soils.

Shred or grind cocoa bean shells before you add them to the compost pile to speed their decomposition. To use them as mulch, spread a layer 1 inch deep around shrubs, evergreens, and flowerbeds. Cocoa shells are also sold at some garden centers.

Before adding seaweed to your compost pile, rinse it off with fresh water to get rid of the salt.

West Coast

The West is the land of plenty when it comes to compostables. It has cotton gin trash, orchard prunings, fish waste, fruit and vegetable pomaces, and more.

Rice hulls. Uncomposted rice hulls aren't especially high in nutrients, but they do add carbon to the compost pile. And compost made with rice hulls is especially good for improving soil tilth and water filtration. Like other high-carbon materials (such as grain straw and nut husks), rice hulls break down faster when composted along with a high-nitrogen material, such as fish waste.

Pomaces. Fruit and vegetable processing wastes—including skin, pulp, seed, and unusable fruits—are usually higher in nutrients and decay much faster than crop residues. You can compost such cannery wastes by themselves or mix them with other organic materials.

Grape pomace from winegrowers is commonly composted with cotton gin trash and manure. And it makes an excellent, disease-fighting compost. In one research project, crops grown in compost made from grape skins and seed (leftover from wine making) resisted soil-borne fungal diseases, including root rot, much better than the same crops grown in a peat mix.

Fish wastes. The West Coast also has tons of fish and wood waste available. Much of the fish waste is used for livestock feed, but shellfish waste is fairly easy to come by. Mix it with wood waste for a nice, well-balanced compost suitable for gardens or container growing.

Seaweed. And let's not forget seaweed! You don't have to visit a cannery, slaughterhouse, or farm to get this well-known organic material. Just gather up a bunch at the tide line along any rocky coast. Seaweed is rich in potassium and micronutrients, such as iron, copper, and zinc. It also contains cytokinins, substances that help your plants grow big and happy. To avoid adding salt to your soil, rinse the seaweed with fresh water before you add it to your compost pile. Seaweed breaks down very fast and should be ready to apply to your soil within a couple of weeks.

MIRACULOUS MUSHROOM COMPOST

ARE THERE ANY mushroom farmers in your area? If so, you can tap their rich supply of mushroom compost—the medium used to grow mushrooms commercially. Mushroom compost (also called "mushroom soil") is a blend of one-third horse manure, one-third spoiled hay, and one-third ground corncobs, with a 1.4-1-1 NPK value and near-neutral pH, making it an excellent amendment for your soil.

Seek out *organic* mushroom compost, however. Organic mushroom compost is steam treated to kill weed seeds, competing fungi, and molds. Others may be chemically treated.

Mushroom growers are plentiful in eastern Pennsylvania, but you can find them in other regions, too. Check with your local Cooperative Extension office for the names of nearby growers.

More than meets the eye: There's a lot going on in your compost pile.

chapter three

Life inside the Compost Pile

Although you may not realize it, a lot is going on in your compost pile. In fact, a compost pile is an intricate and complex community of animal, vegetable, and mineral matter—all working together to break down organic matter into humus.

HELPFUL HUMUS

Composting results from the activities of a succession of organisms, each group paving the way for the next group by breaking down or converting the material at hand into a simpler or more usable material that can be used by the group's successor in the chain.

Whether decomposition takes place on the forest floor or in your compost pile, the process is the same, and humus is always the result.

Humus is a good thing because it's highly beneficial to both the soil and the plants grown in it. Because of its loose texture, humus-rich soil soaks up water so that less runoff occurs. Humus also releases nutrients to plants at a slow enough rate that plants can use them—the nutrients aren't lost through leaching, as are those from chemical fertilizers.

Humus soaks up water and releases nutrients to plants, making it a very good thing.

HOW COMPOST HAPPENS

What happens in a compost pile is similar to what happens in your soil: Microorganisms, nematodes, and earthworms consume organic matter and break it down.

But the transformation of organic matter into finished compost is more complex than that because both chemical and microbial processes are at work.

The First Steps

The process begins with soil microorganisms. They digest the plant and animal materials, causing them to decompose. At the same time, the chemical processes of oxidation, reduction, and hydrolysis are going on in the pile, enhancing breakdown.

Bacteria in the pile obtain energy and nutrients as a result of these processes. Energy comes from the oxidation of materials, especially carbon. Oxidation, or biological "burning," is what causes a compost pile to heat up. Some materials break down and are oxidized more rapidly than others. This explains why a compost pile heats up quickly at the start: Bacteria are attacking these easily decomposed materials and, if all goes well, the materials are soon used. Eventually, the bacterial activity slows down—and the pile begins to cool.

As compost is broken down from raw materials into simpler forms of proteins and carbohydrates, it becomes available as nutrients for a wider array of bacterial species. These bacteria carry the compost to a further stage of decomposition.

Further Decomposition

Carbohydrates (starches and sugars) break down into simple sugars, organic acids, and carbon dioxide that are released into the soil. When proteins decompose, they

A compost pile heats up quickly when you start to make it, then it cools as bacterial activity slows down.

readily break down into peptides and amino acids, and then into available ammonium compounds and atmospheric nitrogen. Finally, bacteria change the ammonium compounds to nitrates—a form that plants can use. At this stage, the pile is almost finished compost, except for a few substances that resist breakdown. Eventually, all of the decomposed organic material in the pile forms humus.

Carbon and Nitrogen

Like other living things, the microorganisms of the compost pile need both carbon from carbohydrates and nitrogen from proteins. In order to thrive and reproduce, the bacteria, actinomycetes, and fungi in the pile also require phosphorus (P), potassium (K), and small amounts of minor elements. But microorganisms can make use of the nitrogen and other elements in the compost pile only when they occur in specific forms and ratios to one another.

The ideal carbon-to-nitrogen (C:N) ratio for most compost microorganisms is about 25:1, but many compost piles have higher or lower ratios—which can cause complications. When too little carbon is present, nitrogen may be lost to microorganisms because they don't have enough carbon to go with it. The nitrogen may float into the atmosphere as ammonia and be lost to the plants that would benefit from its presence in humus. Unpleasant odors from the compost pile are usually caused by nitrogen being released as ammonia.

Materials too high in carbon for the amount of nitrogen present (C:N ratio too high) make composting inefficient, so more time is needed to complete the process. When added to the soil, high-carbon compost uses nitrogen from the soil to continue decomposition, making it unavailable to growing plants. (For more about C:N ratios, see "How to Make Compost" on page 47.)

FUN FACT

BACTERIA "GLUE" TOGETHER PARTICLES OF SOIL, IMPROVING ITS STRUCTURE, MAKING NUTRIENTS MORE AVAILABLE, HOLDING PLANT-FEEDING NITROGEN IN PLACE, AND EVEN DEGRADING POLLUTANTS. THESE 10-MILLIONTH OF AN INCH LONG, SINGLE-CELLED ORGANISMS ARE NEITHER PLANT NOR ANIMAL—SCIENTISTS HAVE CREATED A THIRD KINGDOM JUST FOR THEM.

HELPFUL DECOMPOSERS

Decomposition is at the heart of the composting process, so let's take a closer look at the various organisms involved in this vital function of the working compost pile. Most are microscopic, some are large enough to be observed with the unaided eye, but nearly all are beneficial, each having a role in breaking down raw organic matter into finished compost. They're known as the decomposers.

Microscopic Decomposers

Bacteria are, by far, the most important microscopic decomposers. But there are other microscopic creatures that also play important roles. Together, these microscopic decomposers change the chemistry of the organic wastes, and so are also sometimes called "chemical decomposers."

These decomposers are key to turning waste materials into black gold.

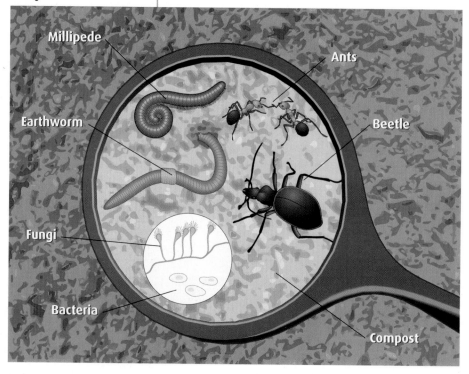

Millipede

Ants

Earthworm

Beetle

Fungi

Bacteria

Compost

ACTINOMYCETES

The characteristically earthy smell of newly plowed soil in the spring is the work of actinomycetes, higher-form bacteria similar to fungi and molds. Actinomycetes are especially important in the formation of humus. Although most bacteria are found in the top foot or so of topsoil, actinomycetes commonly work many feet below the surface. Deep under the roots, they convert dead plant matter into a peatlike substance.

While they are decomposing animal and vegetable matter, actinomycetes free up carbon, nitrogen, and ammonia, making nutrients available for higher plants. Five percent or more of the soil's bacterial population consists of actinomycetes, and most of them are aerobic and mesophilic.

The reason that other bacteria tend to die rapidly as actinomycete populations grow in the compost pile is that actinomycetes produce antibiotics—chemical substances that inhibit bacterial growth.

FUNGI

Fungi are primitive plants that are either single-celled or many-celled and filamentous. Unlike more complex, green plants, they lack chlorophyll and therefore can't make their own carbohydrates. Most of them are classified as saprophytes because they live on dead or dying material and get energy by breaking down organic matter in dead plants and animals.

Like the actinomycetes, fungi take over when the compost pile is in the final stages of decomposition, when the compost has been changed to a more easily digested form. The best temperature for active fungi in the compost heap is around 70° to 75°F (21° to 24°C), though some forms prefer much hotter temperatures and survive to 120°F (49°C).

SOME LIKE IT HOT

THE BENEFICIAL ORGANISMS that inhabit your compost pile roughly fall into two categories: those that thrive in moderate to cool temperatures and those that thrive at higher temperatures. At the beginning of the composting process, mesophilic (medium-temperature) bacteria and fungi predominate. If you checked the temperature of your pile at that point, it probably would be between 50° and 113°F (10° to 45°C).

As the pile becomes hotter (113° to 158°F, or 45° to 70°C), these bacteria give way to thermophilic, or high-temperature, bacteria. The more thermophilic bacteria that are present in the pile—breaking down compounds and releasing heat as a byproduct—the hotter the pile becomes. When things cool down again, the actinomycetes and fungi that had been on the cooler edges of the pile take over, transforming the last bits of raw material into humus.

BACTERIA

The bacteria likely to be found in a compost pile are those that specialize in breaking down organic compounds, those that thrive in temperatures ranging up to 170°F (77°C), and those that are aerobic—needing air to survive. The number of bacteria differ from pile to pile, depending on the materials, temperature, air present, moisture, geographic location, and other factors.

Bacteria are single-celled and can be shaped like spheres, rods, or spiral twists. They're so small that an amount of garden soil the size of a pea could contain up to a million bacteria! Most are colorless and can't make carbohydrates from sunshine, carbon dioxide, and water, the way green plants do.

Bacteria are the most nutritionally diverse of all organisms: As a group they'll eat almost anything. Most compost bacteria, similar to fungi and animals, can use living or dead organic materials. Usually they can produce the appropriate enzyme to digest whatever material they find themselves on.

Because bacteria are smaller, less mobile, and less complex than other organisms, they're less able to escape unfavorable conditions. A decrease in the temperature of the pile or a sharp change in its acidity can kill them or render them inactive.

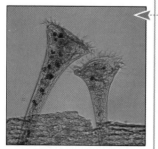

A gram of soil can contain a million protozoa.

PROTOZOA

Protozoa are the simplest form of animal organism. Even though they are single-celled and microscopic, they're larger and more complex than most bacteria. A gram of soil can contain as many as a million protozoa, but compost has far fewer, especially during the thermophilic stage. Protozoa obtain their food from organic matter, the same way bacteria do.

Physical Decomposers

The bacteria, actinomycetes, protozoa, and fungi mostly take care of the chemical decomposition of the compost pile. The larger organisms—such as millipedes, beetles, and ants (known as physical decomposers)—chew and grind their way through the organic materials in the pile.

All of these organisms are part of a complex food chain in your compost pile. They can be categorized as first-, second-, and third-level consumers, depending on what they eat and what eats them. First-level consumers attract and become the food of second-level consumers, which in turn are consumed by third-level consumers. The organisms that make up each level of the food chain serve to keep the populations of the next-lower level in check, so a balance can be maintained throughout the compost pile.

Here are some of the larger physical decomposers that you're likely to find in your compost pile. Most of these creatures function best at medium temperatures, so you won't find them in the pile at all times.

A compost pile is home to lots of different insects and animals. And no matter whether they live at the top of the pile or down below it, they're all key to helping break down the materials you add to your pile.

WHO LIVES WHERE

Life above the compost pile

Fly

Spider

Life inside the compost pile

Beetle

Millipede

Centipede

Slug

Sow bug

Mite

Springtail

Ant

Nematode

Life below the compost pile

Earthworm

Mites are key to making compost, as they help break down plant matter.

MITES

Mites are related to ticks, spiders, and horseshoe crabs because all have eight leglike, jointed appendages. They can be free living or parasitic, sometimes both at once. Some mites are small enough to be invisible to the naked eye, while some tropical species are up to ½ inch long.

Mites reproduce very rapidly, moving through larval, nymph, adult, and dormant stages. They attack plant matter, but some also are second-level consumers, ingesting nematodes, fly larvae, other mites, and springtails.

With a lot of legs to support them, millipedes can make great strides through your pile.

MILLIPEDES

The wormlike body of the millipede has many segments, with the front few bearing two pairs of walking legs. Researchers don't know much about the life cycle of millipedes, other than that millipedes lay their eggs in the soil in springtime, and these eggs hatch into small worms. Young millipedes molt several times before gaining their full complement of legs. When they reach maturity, adult millipedes can grow to a length of 1 to 2 inches. They help break down plant material by feeding directly on it. (Most millipedes protect themselves by spraying a foul-smelling odor at predators.)

Centipedes love to snack on spiders.

CENTIPEDES

Centipedes are flattened, segmented worms with 15 or more pairs of legs—one pair per body segment. They hatch from eggs laid during the warm months and gradually grow into their adult size. These physical decomposers are third-level consumers, feeding only on living animals, especially spiders and insects.

SOW BUGS

Sow bugs are fat-bodied, flat crustaceans (not insects) with distinct segments. These relatives of crabs and lobsters reproduce by means of eggs that hatch into smaller versions of the adults. Because females are able to deposit a number of eggs at one time, sow bugs can become abundant in a compost heap. (Some gardeners who notice them worry that they are pests, but actually they are helping to break down the organic materials into finished compost.) They are first-level consumers, eating decaying vegetation. They use their powerful mouthparts to fragment plant residue and leaf litter.

Female sow bugs are prolific egg layers, filling your compost pile with these decomposers.

SNAILS AND SLUGS

Both snails and slugs are mollusks and have muscular disks on their undersides that are adapted for a creeping movement. Snails have a spirally curved shell, a broad retractable foot, and a distinct head. Slugs, on the other hand, are so undifferentiated in appearance that one species is frequently mistaken for half of a potato! Both snails and slugs lay eggs in capsules or gelatinous masses and progress through larval stages to adulthood.

You're better off with snails in your compost than in your garden.

Their food generally is living plant material, but they'll attack fresh kitchen wastes and plant debris and appear in the compost pile. For that reason, it's a good idea to look for them when you spread your compost. If you spot any, destroy them (drop them into a bucket of soapy water): If they move into your garden, they could multiply and seriously damage plants. (Slugs and snails eat soft, tender plant tissue and make large holes in foliage, stems, and even bulbs. They may also completely demolish seedlings and severely damage young shoots and plants.)

Slugs help break down kitchen wastes in the compost pile.

Spiders help control bad bugs in the garden, as well as help your compost pile.

SPIDERS

Spiders, which are related to mites, are one of the least appreciated animals in the garden—and one of the predators you're most likely to encounter. These eight-legged creatures are third-level consumers that feed on insects and small invertebrates. They can help control garden pests, so solicit their help by leaving them alone when you find them.

Tiny springtails chew on decomposing plants.

SPRINGTAILS

Springtails are very small insects, rarely growing to more than ¼ inch long. They vary in color from white to blue-gray or metallic and are mostly distinguished by their ability to jump when disturbed. They feed by chewing decomposing plants, pollen, and grains. They also scrape and eat bacteria and fungi off of root surfaces. (When feeding on fungi, they help release important plant nutrients.)

This ground beetle preys on snails and insects.

BEETLES

The rove beetle, ground beetle, and feather-winged beetle are the most common beetles in compost. Feather-winged beetles feed on fungal spores, and the larger rove and ground beetles prey on other insects as third-level consumers.

Beetles are easily visible insects with two pairs of wings. The front pair serve as a cover or shield for the thinner back wings, which are used for flying.

Most adult beetles, like the larval grubs of their species, feed on decaying vegetables; others, like the rove and ground beetles, prey on snails, insects, and other small animals. The black rove beetle preys on snails and slugs. Some people bring them into their gardens when slugs become a problem.

ANTS

Ants feed on various materials, including aphid honeydew, fungi, seeds, sweets, scraps, other insects, and sometimes other ants. Compost provides some of these foods as well as shelter for nests and hills. But ants will remain in the compost pile only while the pile is relatively cool.

Ants prey on first-level consumers and may benefit the composting process by bringing fungi and other organisms into their nests. The work of ants can make compost richer in phosphorus and potassium by moving minerals from one place to another.

Compost supplies food as well as shelter for ants.

FLIES

Many flies—including black fungus gnats, soldier flies, minute flies, and houseflies—spend their larval phase in compost as maggots. Adults can feed on almost any kind of organic material.

All flies undergo egg, larval, pupal, and adult stages. The eggs are laid in various forms of organic matter. Houseflies are such effective distributors of bacteria that when an individual fly crawls across a sterile plate of lab gelatin, colonies of bacteria later appear in its tracks. During the early phases of the composting process, flies provide ideal airborne transportation for bacteria on their way to the compost pile.

If you keep a layer of dry leaves on top of your pile and cover any kitchen scraps promptly when building compost, your pile won't provide a breeding ground for horseflies, mosquitoes, or houseflies, which may become a nuisance to humans. Fly larvae can't survive thermophilic temperatures. Mites in the pile also keep fly larvae reduced in number. Though many flies die when frost arrives, their reproduction rate is so fast that a few survivors can repopulate an area quickly when the weather warms up.

If you cover kitchen scraps promptly when adding them to your pile, it won't provide a breeding ground for flies.

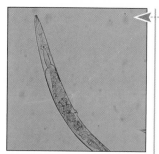

Helpful nematodes live on decaying material in your compost pile.

NEMATODES, FLATWORMS, AND ROTIFERS

Nematodes, or eelworms, plus free-living flatworms, and rotifers can all take up residence in a compost pile.

Nematodes are microscopic creatures that can be classified into three categories:

- Those that live on decaying organic matter
- Those that are predators of other nematodes, bacteria, algae, protozoa, and so on
- Those that can be serious pests in gardens, where they attack plant roots

Flatworms, as their name implies, are flattened organisms that are usually quite small in their free-living form. Most flatworms are carnivorous. They live in films of water within the compost pile.

Rotifers are small, muticelled animals that live freely or in tubes attached to a substrate. Their bodies are round and divisible into three parts: head, trunk, and tail. They're generally found in films of water, and many forms are aquatic. The rotifers in compost are found in water that adheres to plant substances, where they feed on microorganisms.

The earthworm's main purpose in life is to till and enrich the soil in your yard and garden.

EARTHWORMS

If bacteria are the champion microscopic decomposers, then the heavyweight champion is the earthworm, which no other creature can match when it comes to tilling and enriching the soil.

The earthworm consists mainly of an alimentary canal that ingests, decomposes, and deposits casts continually during the earthworm's active periods. As soil or organic matter is passed through an earthworm's digestive system, it's broken up and neutralized by secretions of calcium carbonate from glands near the worm's gizzard. Once in the gizzard, material is finely ground before it's digested.

Digestive intestinal juices rich in hormones, enzymes, and other fermenting substances continue the breakdown process. The organic matter passes out of the worm's body in the form of casts, which are the richest and finest quality of all humus material. Fresh casts are considerably higher in bacteria, organic material, and available nitrogen, calcium, magnesium, phosphorus, and potassium than soil itself. Earthworms thrive on compost and contribute to its quality through both physical and chemical processes.

Because earthworms are so important to compost making, smart gardeners adjust their composting methods to take full advantage of the earthworm's many talents. (You'll read more about how to do this in "How to Make Compost" on page 47.)

BY THE NUMBERS

EARTHWORMS ARE incredibly important to good garden soil—so when you add compost that contains some earthworms to your beds, you're giving your soil an added bonus.

But because those worms work out of sight, you might not be sure just how many worms are down below—and whether your soil could use some more. To get an estimate of the earthworm population, dig a hole 8 to 10 inches deep and 1 foot wide, and count the number of earthworms you find in the soil you remove. More than 10 earthworms is great, and 6 to 10 indicates a moderately healthy soil. But if you have fewer than 5, you need to do some serious work. This low number could be an indication of low organic matter, pH problems, and/or poor drainage.

If your earthworm count is low, don't despair. Once you provide more organic material to feed them, they'll return. Healthy soil can contain about 1.5 million worms per acre—even more reason not to underestimate the importance of these ambitious decomposers. And if you think that number sounds surprisingly high, consider that worms multiply extremely quickly—producing upward of 2,000 to 3,000 offspring per worm per year!

You don't have to put a lot of effort into making compost—but the rewards will be tremendous.

chapter four

How to Make Compost

Composting isn't difficult. All you need are some raw ingredients, a tool for handling the compost, and a place to pile it. The organisms in the pile do most of the work for you—so you end up with a great (and free) soil amendment without having to put a lot of effort into it.

RECIPE FUNDAMENTALS

The basic principles of composting are simple: Combine your ingredients to provide a good nutritional balance, keep the pile well-aerated and moist (not soggy), and let the compost microorganisms do the rest. An active compost pile, turned once a week or so, will heat up inside to a temperature as high as 160°F, but if you're willing to wait for your finished compost, you don't even have to turn it. How much easier could it get?

The compost pile has its own ecosystem, with various organisms playing a central role during different steps of the cycle. As the pile heats up, mesophilic bacteria—those that prefer some warmth—proliferate. When temperatures get above 120°F, thermophilic, or heat-loving, organisms do more of the work. At cooler temperatures, fungi and actinomycetes predominate. Earthworms and other visible macroorganisms do their jobs at cooler temperatures and on the edges of the heating pile.

You can choose from a wide selection of materials and methods to compost successfully. But the same basic principles apply to all of them. When you understand what the microbes need to flourish, you'll know what to do to help make compost happen. Before you know it, you'll have your own supply of "black gold."

If you provide the right balance of ingredients for your compost pile and keep it well aerated and moist, the compost microorganisms will do the rest.

CARBON-TO-NITROGEN RATIO OF ORGANIC MATERIALS

MATERIALS WITH a carbon-to-nitrogen (C:N) ratio of 30:1 or lower are considered to be high in nitrogen, while materials with a higher C:N ratio are considered high in carbon.

Material	C:N Ratio	Material	C:N Ratio
Vegetable wastes	12:1	Dry leaves	50:1
Alfalfa hay	13:1	Cornstalks	60:1
Grass clippings	19:1	Grain hulls/chaff	80:1
Seaweed	19:1	Straw	80:1
Rotted manure	20:1	Timothy hay	80:1
Apple pomace	21:1	Sugarcane fiber	200:1
Pea or bean shells	30:1	Sawdust	400:1

COMPOSTING BASICS

The aim of every composting method is simply to meet the needs of the microorganisms that do the work of turning raw organic matter into humus. Those basic needs are energy food (carbon) and protein food (nitrogen) in the right proportion; air; moisture; and warmth. A pile also needs to be a minimum size so that high enough temperatures can be maintained.

Feed the Decomposers

The first step to successful composting is providing the right mixture of basic ingredients. Raw organic matter, the basic food for compost organisms, consists of carbohydrates (carbon) and proteins (nitrogen) in differing proportions. To keep the decomposers well-fed, you need to provide these two food groups in the right balance.

Carbohydrates, which provide energy and cell-building compounds, must make up the bulk of the diet. Protein, which is essential for growth and reproduction, is needed in much smaller quantities. A ratio of 20 to 30 parts carbon to 1 part nitrogen is ideal.

In general, carbon materials are brown or yellow and dry, bulky, or fluffy (that's why they're commonly referred to as the "dry browns"). Dry leaves, straw, hay, and sawdust are all high in carbon.

Nitrogen materials tend to be green and wet, succulent, dense, or sticky, which is why they're often called "wet greens." Fresh manure, grass clippings, fish wastes, and soybean meal are rich in nitrogen.

Keep the Pile Moist

Your compost pile should be about as moist as a damp sponge. If you can squeeze water out of it, it's too wet. But the moisture level of your compost pile shouldn't be much of a problem if you're mixing the right proportions of dry carbon materials with wet nitrogen ones.

Here are some other ways to regulate the moisture level in your compost.

- For most areas, make sure your pile is in a well-drained site. For very arid regions, however, consider digging a shallow composting pit to trap more moisture.

If your compost pile dries out, spray it with water until it's the consistency of a damp sponge.

- If your ingredients are dry, sprinkle each layer with a hose or watering can until everything is moist and has a good sheen.

- Shape your pile according to your climate. In a wet climate, round the top to shed rain. In a dry climate, make a shallow depression on top to trap water.

- To shed excess rainwater and protect the compost materials from the drying effects of the sun and wind, cover the pile with a little loose hay or straw, or use dark plastic. Or, make your compost in a container with a lid.

At the end of the growing season, save spent cornstalks and use them to aerate your compost pile.

Aerate the Pile

Most home compost piles depend on aerobic organisms, which require air to live. So proper aeration is critical to successful composting.

To make sure your pile is well aerated, start by choosing a well-drained site. Compost that sits in a puddle, even for a short time, will wick up the water into essential air spaces in the pile.

You'll also need to provide air passages beneath the pile. Layer brush, spent cornstalks, or other coarse materials at the bottom of the pile. Or, make a wire mesh bottom for your compost bin so that it sits a couple of inches above the ground.

The bulky carbon materials you use in your compost pile create air passages throughout the pile, improving air flow and supplying food. Straw is highly valued for this reason. But be careful about using large layers of leaves, paper, grass clippings, or other ingredients that tend to mat when wet. Before adding these materials to your pile, shred them to fluff them up a bit and to prevent them from matting together.

Turning is the traditional way to aerate compost, and frequent turning is the key to quick, hot compost. The more often you turn the pile, the faster the raw materials will decompose and the higher the temperatures will become.

Size Up the Pile

Composting works best when the temperature inside the pile remains at about 140°F or higher. Things heat up fast with the right mix of materials, air, and water. But to keep things cooking, you need the pile to be of a certain size—at least 3 × 3 × 3 feet—to provide the necessary mass.

If the pile is smaller than that, the heat will dissipate before the pile can reach the right temperature for the thermophilic organisms. A pile that's much larger than that will be difficult for you to turn, and the interior can become anaerobic. Instead of making a pile that's too large, make two medium-sized ones.

Bacteria begin to go dormant and compost stops cooking when the compost temperature drops below 55°F. But with a properly built compost pile, the interior temperature will stay well above that—even in freezing weather. Northern gardeners sometimes insulate their piles with leaves, straw, or even an enclosure of hay bales to keep things cooking in cold weather. Decomposition may slow for the winter but should speed up again and finish during the warmer months of spring.

DO YOU NEED A COMPOST INOCULANT?

WILL USING ONE of the bacterial "compost starter" inoculants give you compost faster? No, say university researchers. According to recent tests, raw compost materials already contain more than enough bacteria to get your compost mixture cooking.

The researchers performed their tests on four compost piles, all containing a typical backyard compost mix of 2 parts leaves to 1 part grass clippings.

One pile received a standard commercial inoculant; the second, a "premium" commercial inoculant; the third, some year-old compost; and the fourth, no inoculant. All four compost piles were turned and watered weekly, and all heated up to 130°F. At the end of 2 months, all four piles contained equally finished compost. The university researchers concluded that the inoculants offered no benefit to a typical grass and leaves compost pile.

5 STEPS TO QUICK COMPOST

Raking up some fallen leaves in a corner of your yard and gradually adding garden wastes and kitchen scraps is a simple, low-tech way to compost. This laissez-faire method makes what's called "cool compost" because the pile literally stays cool. (We'll tell you more about cold versus hot compost on page 54.) Just let the pile sit, and in about a year, you'll have sweet-smelling, dark brown, crumbly compost.

You may have seen your neighbors turning their compost piles and watering them. Why do they do these things? Because they want compost fast—from start to finish in just a month. So they make an active, or *hot*, compost pile. The microorganisms that drive the composting process need a steady supply of water and air, and the more they get, the faster they work.

There are five key steps in making a hot compost pile. The more you're willing to work with your compost, the faster it'll decompose.

1. **Shred and chop.** Shred or chop materials as finely as you can before mixing them into your pile. For example, you can chop fallen leaves by running your lawn mower over them. The same strategy applies to kitchen scraps and the like—"the smaller the better" is always the rule for compost ingredients.

Use your lawn mower to chop leaves into fine pieces before adding them to your compost pile.

2. **Mix dry browns and wet greens.** The two basic types of ingredients for making compost are those rich in carbon and those rich in nitrogen. Carbon-rich materials, or "dry browns," include leaves, hay, and straw. Nitrogen-rich materials, or "wet greens," include kitchen scraps and grass clippings (which work best when used sparsely and mixed in well so they don't mat down). Your goal is to keep a fair mix of these materials throughout your pile. (If you try to make compost solely with wet greens or dry browns, you won't have much luck.)

3. **Strive for size.** Build your pile at least 3 × 3 × 3 to 4 feet so materials will heat up and decompose quickly. (Remember, though, not to make your pile too big, or else it will be hard for you to turn.) Unless you have this critical mass of materials, your compost pile can't really get cooking. Check the pile a couple of days after you make it—it should be hot in the middle, a sign that your microbial decomposers are working hard.

An ideal size for a compost pile is about 3 × 3 × 3 feet.

Help get air into your pile by mixing things up with a pitchfork.

4. Add water as needed. Make sure your pile stays moist, but not too wet (it should look like a damp sponge). You may need to add water occasionally.

5. Keep things moving. Moving your compost adds air to the mix. One way to add air is to get in there with a pitchfork and open up air holes. Even better, move the entire pile over a few feet bit by bit, taking care to move what was on the outside to the inside of the new pile and vice versa. Or consider getting a compost tumbler—a container that moves the materials for you. A less labor-intensive way to add air is to put a homemade "chimney" in the center of the pile. (For more on low-effort aeration, see "Easier Aeration" on the opposite page.)

COMPOST: HOT OR COLD?

There's more than one way to make compost. The best method for you depends on many factors, such as the time and effort you're able to give, the space you have available, and the amount of compost you need. Composting methods range from quick, hot composting that requires more effort and attention (as described on page 52) to slow, cool techniques that are less trouble. Both hot and cold composting have advantages and drawbacks.

Hot Stuff

The biggest advantage of hot composting is its fast turnover—generally less than 8 weeks and as few as 2 weeks. To achieve that fast breakdown, the pile needs aeration: The more air it gets, the hotter it becomes (and the more hospitable to thermophilic bacteria). The object is to maintain a temperature of 113° to 158°F until decomposition is complete. You can use a thermometer to monitor the temperature or simply feel the inside of the pile with your hand. If it feels hot to the touch, you're in the ballpark. But when the temperature drops below this range, you must turn the ingredients to get the process going again.

With hot composting, you can process six or more batches in one season, even in cool climates. If you need lots of compost but have limited room to produce it, this is the way to go.

The other major advantage to hot compost is its temperature. Few weed seeds and pathogens can survive thermophilic temperatures, especially if they're maintained for several weeks.

The major disadvantage of hot composting is the labor required. Not everyone is willing or able to turn the pile every few days. Hot compost also demands specific conditions: If the moisture level or carbon-to-nitrogen ratio is wrong, you have to make adjustments. Another drawback is that you have to build the whole pile at one time. If you don't have the materials on hand to make a pile of the proper size, you must accumulate and store them until you're ready to build a new pile.

Finally, hot compost usually contains less nitrogen than cold compost. Turning allows more nitrogen to escape into the air in the form of ammonia gas.

EASIER AERATION

YOU CAN GET air into the center of your compost pile without turning it at all! The trick is to run ventilation pipes—perforated PVC pipes—through the pile. (If you don't have PVC pipes on hand, you can substitute cornstalks or palm fronds—both of these plants have an open center.)

You'll need several pipes that are about 4 feet long, or a little longer than the width or height of your pile. Run one pipe horizontally through the middle of the pile. Insert parallel pipes vertically about 6 inches away, on either side of the middle pipe. As the pile heats up, withdraw a pipe and reinsert it in another part of the pile. Do this every few days, if possible.

Another easy way to open air channels without turning is simply to stab the pile with a pitchfork once a week or so.

HOT VERSUS COOL: COMPOST PROS & CONS

Hot Pros

- Produces finished compost quickly
- Uses space efficiently
- Kills most weed seeds and pathogens

Hot Cons

- Labor intensive
- Requires careful control of moisture and carbon-to-nitrogen ratio
- Requires enough materials to build a 3 × 3 × 3-foot pile at one time
- May contain less nitrogen
- Doesn't contain as many disease-fighting organisms

Cool Pros

- Needs little maintenance
- Spares disease-fighting microbes
- Conserves nitrogen
- Allows for materials to be added gradually

Cool Cons

- Takes 6 months to 2 years to produce finished compost
- Doesn't kill pathogens or weed seeds
- Needs a balance of carbon and nitrogen materials to be added to the pile
- Contains more pieces of high-carbon materials that haven't decomposed
- May lose nutrients because of extended exposure to rain and sun

Studies also have shown that compost produced at high temperatures is less able to suppress soil-borne diseases than cool compost. That's because the beneficial bacteria and fungi that attack pathogens can't survive the higher temperatures.

The Cool Alternative

If you have the space but not the time or stamina to play with your compost, you can take the passive approach and make "cool compost." Cool compost will still heat up at first, but it won't reach the high temperature that actively turned compost will. The maximum temperature of cool compost is about 120°F. At that temperature, the mesophilic organisms do most of the work of making humus, which will be complete in 6 months to 2 years, depending on climate, materials, and aeration.

The advantages and disadvantages of cool composting mirror those of hot composting. Cool composting takes less work, but you'll need to wait longer to get the finished product. Cool composting also fails to kill pathogens or weed seeds but spares disease-fighting microbes.

One big plus of cool compost is that it can contain more nitrogen than hot compost. Some research has shown that "no-turn" compost contains as much as 13 percent more nitrogen than composts that are turned twice a week. In an unturned pile, microbes convert nitrogen into a stable form, so less escapes into the air as ammonia gas. To maintain that higher nitrogen level, however, you *must* cover your compost to protect it from rain. Otherwise, much of the nitrogen will leach away in the rainwater.

Another advantage of cool composting is that you can add materials a little at a time, as you accumulate them. The drawback is that you must be careful to balance carbon and nitrogen materials as you go, or you risk creating anaerobic conditions (which can cause an unpleasant odor). To prevent that from happening, keep a supply of dry carbon materials on hand to layer in when you add kitchen scraps or grass clippings.

To build a cool compost pile, follow these steps.

1. First lay a base of brush on a well-drained site.

2. Add ingredients as you accumulate them, keeping a good mix of carbon and nitrogen materials. As you add new materials, moisten them lightly, if needed, and cover them with a bit of soil.

3. When the pile has reached 3 × 3 × 3 feet, cover it with a layer of straw or leaves and let it rest for 6 months to a year, or more.

4. Before using, screen out any pieces that haven't decomposed.

quick tip

Compost camouflage: To conceal your work in progress, plant a border of fast-growing annuals, such as sunflowers, tall cosmos, or nicotiana, in front of your compost.

THE LOWDOWN ON MANURE

Farmers and gardeners have been fertilizing their soil with animal manure for centuries, and animal manure has long been recommended as a good source of nitrogen for compost piles, too. After all, animal manure is a rich source of soil nutrients, and it adds precious organic matter to soil. But for all the benefits that animal manure can offer your garden, it has a big drawback: Some may contain toxic bacteria.

Keeping It Out of Your Pile

If you add fresh animal manure to your compost pile, you run the risk of contaminating it with a virulent strain of *Escherichia coli* bacteria: *E. coli* 0157:H7. This bacteria lives in the intestines of cows and some other animals and appears in their manure. We humans have *E. coli* in our stomachs, too, but *E. coli* 0157 is a new, dangerous form that produces a toxin that can cause severe illness, especially in small children, the elderly, and people with compromised immune systems.

Play it safe and avoid using Bossy's by-products in your pile—unless you're certain your compost will heat up to over 140°F.

So until scientists learn more about this new strain of *E. coli*, you may want to avoid using raw manure in your home compost pile, unless you are *certain* that your compost will heat up to over 140°F (the temperature needed to kill off harmful pathogens).

The good news, though, is that you don't need manure to make compost. Fresh grass clippings are an excellent, readily available, alternative source of nitrogen that you can add to your compost pile. Vegetable-type kitchen scraps are usually a good source of nitrogen as well. And alfalfa and soybean meals (available at farm supply stores) are just two examples of commercial products you can purchase to give your compost pile a boost of nitrogen.

Never spread manure over vegetable gardens that have already been planted, and don't use pet feces in your pile—dogs and cats can carry parasites that, in rare cases, can be transmitted to humans (see page 60). And always wash your hands well after working in the garden—as well as any fresh produce you harvested.

WHAT NOT TO PUT IN THE COMPOST PILE

Although you *can* compost nearly any organic material, you should avoid or limit the use of certain materials, such as the following:

Meat scraps. These can attract unwanted animal visitors and create unpleasant odors.

Fats, oils, and grease. Large amounts of fats, oils, or grease will give your microbes indigestion, slowing down the composting process. They also may attract rodents and other pests.

Droppings from caged birds. Bird droppings may contain dangerous disease pathogens. And because they're mixed with bedding and dropped birdseed from the bottom of the cage, these droppings also can introduce weed seeds into your compost.

SHREDDING SECRET

MANY GARDENERS BELIEVE that the secret to fast compost is to start with small pieces. Prunings, cornstalks, and other large materials won't break down as fast as other materials in the pile—and probably will just get in your way—unless you shred them first.

One reader of *Organic Gardening* magazine has his shredding down to a science. On weekends, he collects weeds, prunings, spent vines, dry leaves, and grass clippings from his property and then runs everything through a chipper/shredder. He then makes a pile out of the shredded materials or adds them to an existing pile. About a month later—after the pile has heated and cooled—he spreads the resulting compost out to dry for a few days. Then, the *pièce de résistance:* He runs it through the chipper/shredder a *second* time. The finished product is moist and fluffy and ready to use.

Droppings from dogs, cats, or other carnivores. These could contain disease organisms harmful to humans. Hot composting kills most pathogens, but some may be able to survive even prolonged heat. Cat droppings, in particular, can be hazardous to pregnant women and small children. These droppings may contain *Toxoplasma gondii*, a one-celled organism that can infect an unborn child, causing brain and eye disease. *Toxocara cati*, a roundworm common in cat droppings, can cause similar problems in children. Avoid these problems by keeping the litter box away from the compost pile and children.

Human waste. The potential for spreading disease makes the use of human waste in the compost pile too risky.

Diseased plants. Yes, hot composting kills most plant pathogens. But why risk it? Instead, burn diseased plants and add their ashes to the compost pile. Or send them to the landfill.

Weeds. Weeds that have set seed can cause trouble unless your pile is hot enough to kill the seeds. Better not to risk contaminating your whole garden with them. Certain weeds should be kept out of the compost pile entirely. Canada thistle, quack grass, couch grass, John-

Dog feces can contain harmful disease organisms, so keep canine droppings out of your pile.

songgrass, bishop's weed, comfrey, and Jerusalem artichokes can all reproduce easily from the tiniest bit of surviving root or rhizome.

Allelopathic plants. Some plants contain chemical compounds that inhibit the growth of other plants. In time, most of these compounds break down during the compost process. But to be on the safe side, you might want to avoid composting any materials from these plants, which include black walnut, sunflowers, and eucalyptus.

Large or slow-to-decompose materials. Large pieces of wood, bones, oyster and clam shells, rags, brush, cornstalks, heavy cardboard, and the like will just get in the way. If you want to compost them, shred or crush them first to speed their decay.

Highly acidic materials. If you want to use materials that are very acidic, such as fruit pomaces, add some crushed limestone to the pile to neutralize the acid. *Exception:* For acid-loving plants, such as azaleas and blueberries, you might *want* an acidic compost. In that case, skip the limestone.

KEEPING TOXINS OUT

What about those widely available but questionable materials, such as floral shop waste or grass clippings from neighbors and golf courses? If the materials have been treated with herbicides or insecticides, can you poison your compost and garden by adding them to your pile?

These are good questions. Unfortunately, there are no easy answers. According to the University of Illinois Center for Solid Waste Management Research, some commonly used herbicides can remain active for a full year.

And a researcher at the Connecticut Agricultural Experiment Station says crops can take up some of these herbicides after the herbicides have been introduced

DON'T CONTAMINATE YOUR COMPOST!

MOST ORGANIC WASTES make good compost fodder, but some materials are likely to contain toxic residues (herbicides, pesticides, fungicides, or heavy metals) that could contaminate your compost and your garden. Keep these out of your compost pile:

- Grass clippings from neighbors or businesses that use herbicides
- Grass clippings from golf courses
- Highway trimmings
- Florist shop wastes
- Leather meal
- Cottonseed meal (unless from an organic farm)
- Paper mill sludge
- Coal ash
- Sewage sludge
- Municipal incinerator ash

HOW TO MAKE COMPOST   61

to the garden. So, theoretically, you could get traces of these toxins in the food you grow.

Scientific research on how pesticides and herbicides break down in the compost pile is just beginning. But the consensus is that some of these substances may survive the composting process. Whether they do or not depends on which pesticide or herbicide was used—different chemicals break down at different rates. And the conditions within the compost pile (such as heat, moisture, and pH) also affect the rate at which they disappear.

Don't add golf course trimmings to your compost pile, unless you're certain they haven't been treated with chemicals.

Avoiding Tainted Compost

With all of these variables, there's just no way for the average home gardener to tell when (or if) compost ingredients that started out tainted become safe for organic food growing. So the answer for true organic gardeners is "no"—just don't do it. Don't add any herbicide- or pesticide-treated materials to your compost pile.

In case this warning comes too late and you've already added some treated golf course trimmings to your pile, don't despair. You can speed up the breakdown process and get rid of toxic residues as fast as possible (and more completely) by revving up the composting process.

According to an Ohio State University researcher, herbicide and insecticide molecules are more readily degraded under aerobic conditions. And the best way to achieve those conditions? Turn, turn, turn. The more often you turn your compost pile, the more air you add, and the faster the herbicides and pesticides will break down.

COMPOSTING TECHNIQUES AND RECIPES

It's no secret that there are plenty of different ways to compost. As long as you use the right ingredients—chopped or shredded "dry browns," "wet greens," air, moisture, and time—any method will work.

Here are several tried-and-true methods and a few new recipes that some ingenious gardeners concocted. Try a couple on for size, then choose the best one for you—or devise your own variation. You can't go wrong!

Good Old Grass and Leaves

One of the simplest techniques for making good-quality compost requires only four ingredients: dry leaves, fresh grass clippings, water, and soil.

1. Collect dry leaves and some fresh grass clippings.

2. Mix two to four buckets of clippings with 10 buckets of leaves.

3. As you work, spray the materials with a hose so that the mix feels wet, but not soggy, when you touch it. Also, add a shovelful of good garden soil as you go to introduce friendly composting bacteria to the pile.

4. Repeat Steps 2 and 3 until your pile is finished.

If you turn this mix weekly and add more water if the pile starts to dry out, you should have rich, beautiful compost in just 1 to 2 months.

Garbage Can Compost

No space in your yard for a big compost pile? Then make compost in a can. Use a sturdy plastic or metal garbage can. Punch several holes in the bottom and sides of the can. Stand the can on bricks set in a large pan (to catch any liquid that might drain out). Layer 3 inches of soil, 2 to 3 inches of kitchen scraps, and then 2 inches of grass clippings, shredded newspapers, or

COMPOST INGREDIENTS

High-Carbon "Dry Browns"

Dry leaves

Dry weeds

Straw

Hay

Chopped cornstalks

Aged sawdust

Nutshells

Paper (moderate amounts)

High-Nitrogen "Wet Greens"

Vegetable scraps

Fruit scraps

Coffee grounds

Tea bags

Fresh grass clippings

Fresh leaves (avoid walnut and eucalyptus)

Freshly pulled weeds

Hair (pet and human)

Manure (cow, poultry, horse, pig, rabbit)

Seaweed

chopped leaves. Repeat the layers until the can is full, finishing with a layer of soil. The finished compost will be ready in about 3 to 4 months—with no turning required! One caution: With this method, the compost may produce odors as it breaks down, so put the can in an out-of-the-way spot.

Stockpile materials for your compost tumbler until you have enough to fill it two-thirds full.

Terrific Tumbler Compost

The secret to success with a tumbler is to stockpile materials until you have enough to almost fill the tumbler. Here's the technique:

1. Start stockpiling kitchen wastes in a 20-gallon garbage can (put the can right by your tumbler). In about 2 weeks, you should have enough for a batch of compost.

2. Transfer the kitchen wastes to the tumbler drum, and then add equal volumes of chopped leaves and grass clippings.

3. Rotate the tumbler a few times every day for 2 weeks. (You should also be stockpiling a new batch of kitchen wastes during this time.)

4. Unload the finished compost and load in new materials to start the next cycle.

When you reach October, you can load the tumbler one final time. That batch will be ready at about the end of the following April, and you can begin the 2-week routine again.

Blender Booster

To jump-start your compost pile, whiz up a batch of "liquid compost." As kitchen scraps accumulate, put them in a blender, add just enough water to cover them, then blend until finely chopped. Pour the resulting liquid into a bucket with a lid.

When you're ready to add it to your compost pile, dig a shallow hole into the center of the pile, then pour in the liquid. Cover the mixture with a shovelful of compost.

Or, if your gardening space is limited and you don't have room to make a traditional compost pile, pour the liquid gold directly into trenches dug in the garden. Cover with a shovelful of dirt.

Sheet Composting

Another way to make compost without a traditional compost pile is to use the "sheet" method: Your garden beds serve as your compost pile. The idea is to clean up the bed at the end of the season, spread yard and garden waste over the bed, and then dig it all in.

By spring, your bed will be rich with compost. But because you lose the benefit of a heap's heat, you must be extra careful about the materials you use. Don't bury any diseased plants or weeds that have gone to seed. And, if you use kitchen scraps, bury them at least 8 inches deep so critters won't dig them up.

Follow these five steps to successful sheet composting in your garden:

1. Collect your yard waste. Remove large stalks and dense, fibrous matter, and then place the rest on the bed you've chosen.

2. Shred the material or run a lawn mower over it.

3. Add some high-nitrogen material, such as grass clippings or manure. Mix it all together.

NO SPACE TO COMPOST? TRY TRENCHES

IF YOU DON'T have room for a compost pile, you may find that trench composting is the best way to add nutrients to your soil. How do you trench compost? Just dig a hole in your garden every day, about 8 inches deep, and bury kitchen scraps. If you start along one side of a garden row, you'll actually be side-dressing or fertilizing nearby vegetables as well as boosting soil texture and fertility for next season.

You shouldn't have a problem with animals digging up what you've buried if you avoid adding meat, fat, and bones. If dogs do begin to dig in your trenches, just use a roll of chicken wire to cover your buried treasure. Roll it out over one hole at a time, along the row. Because the roll moves gradually, it also marks where you buried something last.

The first step in sheet composting is to collect yard waste, including spent leaves.

4. Work the mixture into the top foot of soil, using a spade or tiller.

5. Turn the soil again in spring.

Three-Bin Composting

If you have a three-bin composter (see "Tools and Supplies" on page 13), you can cook up a steady supply of compost for your soil. The following week-by-week schedule will help you get the most from your composter. Remember to check the moisture content when you transfer compost from bin to bin. Add dry material if it seems too soggy and water if it seems too dry.

Week 1: In the center bin, build a traditional compost pile (such as described in "Good Old Grass and Leaves" on page 63). Spread a base layer of dry leaves or straw in the holding bin on one side; toss in kitchen wastes or garden trimmings as you collect them.

Weeks 2 and 3: Remove a few front boards from the center bin and stir the compost. Keep adding to the holding bin.

Week 4: Remove all front boards from the bins. Using a fork, transfer the compost from the center bin to the empty bin. Then transfer the contents of the holding bin to the now-empty center bin. Spread a new layer of dry matter in the now-empty holding bin. Replace the front boards.

Week 5: Check the compost in the end bin. It should be ready to use.

Cold-Weather Composting

When the weather turns cold in the fall, you can still keep your compost pile working by insulating it. Simply gather bags of fallen leaves from the curbsides around your town and heap them in a circle about 4 feet in diameter around a low compost pile. The bags provide some heat, the contents of the bags will decompose slightly, and the center of the circle should stay unfrozen all winter, so you can keep dumping your kitchen scraps there.

You can also insulate a compost bin by piling straw bales around it and covering the whole thing with a large sheet of plastic.

The arrival of Old Man Winter doesn't mean you have to stop composting—you'll just need to insulate your bin.

BREW SOME COMPOST TEA

RECENT RESEARCH has confirmed what many organic gardeners have known for years: "Compost tea" is a potent stimulant for plants. As always, the beneficial effect starts with the soil, where humic acids in the tea stimulate biological activity. In one study, compost tea increased beneficial soil microbes by 500 percent. And in turn, plant growth increased by an astounding 700 percent!

To make your own batch of compost tea, simply fill a container one-quarter of the way with compost. Add water to almost fill the container, then stir a few times over the next day. To use the tea, dilute it to a light amber color. Pour a pint around each plant that you set out in the garden. During the growing season, use it to feed garden and houseplants every 10 to 14 days.

LET WORMS DO THE WORK

DID YOU KNOW that you can compost even in an apartment? Keep earthworms in a box, feed them your kitchen scraps, and watch them turn your garbage into rich, black humus. If you're careful about constructing and maintaining the box, composting with worms (or vermicomposting) is virtually odor-free.

Make sure you get the right worms for the job. Redworms (*Lumbricus rubellus*) or manure worms (*Eisenia fetida*) work best. These worms can process large amounts of organic material, they reproduce well in culture, and they tolerate a range of temperatures. You aren't likely to find them in your garden, though. You'll have to buy them from a fish bait supplier or mail-order garden supplier. Most vermicomposting systems use 1 to 2 pounds of worms (that's 1,200 to 2,400 of them).

Besides the worms, you'll need a container, shredded newspaper and garden soil for bedding, a steady supply of kitchen wastes, and the right environment.

For an average home, a suitable size worm box is about 2 × 2 × 1 foot. You can buy a commercially available worm bin or make your own, using untreated lumber. A plastic storage bin of about the same dimensions will work fine, too. But no matter what type of container you use, make sure it has holes in the bottom for aeration and drainage. Drill at least six ⅛-inch holes in the bottom and some more holes around the sides.

Worm Care and Feeding

The next step is to prepare the bedding for your worms. Just take a section of black and white newspaper and tear it into 1½-inch wide strips. Mix together 1 part shredded paper with 3 parts water and a handful of garden soil. Put the damp bedding in the bottom of the worm bin.

Add 1 pound of worms—they'll disappear immediately into the bedding. Add 1 to 2 pounds of kitchen waste, burying it into the bedding. After a week or so, the worms will be able to process larger amounts. In a typical 2 × 2-foot bin, a pound of redworms can process about 3½ pounds of organic waste each week. Each time you add kitchen scraps, bury them in a new location to avoid odors.

Loosely cover the bin with a lid or sheet of plastic to maintain the proper humidity.

After 2 to 3 months, you can harvest the worm castings—the nutrient-rich droppings, or compost. Push the castings to one side of the box, then add fresh bedding and kitchen wastes to the other side. For 2 to 4 weeks, add wastes to the fresh side only to encourage the worms to leave the finished compost. When they move, remove the rest of the compost, and add fresh bedding.

Worm Nutrition

Here are some suggestions for your worms' diet:

Do Feed Your Worms	Don't Feed Your Worms
Bread	Animal products
Coffee filters	Butter
Coffee grounds	Cheese
Eggshells	Fish
Fruit rinds	Casseroles with oil
Grains	Meat
Tea bags	
Vegetable scraps	

TROUBLESHOOTING

Because compost is so integral to organic gardening, the creation of a "perfect" pile is a goal to which many gardeners aspire. But what if your results are less than perfect?

Don't throw in the towel. Here are some common compost problems and what to do about them.

Wet, Soggy, Slimy Compost

Nothing is worse than cold, slimy compost! How does it get this way? Usually there are three contributing factors: poor aeration, too much moisture, and/or not enough nitrogen-rich materials in the compost pile.

A compost pile that is overburdened with materials that mat down when wet—such as grass clippings, spoiled hay, and unshredded leaves—can become so dense that the pile's center receives no air. If you leave this pile uncovered during prolonged rain (and don't turn it to introduce some air into the center), you'll end up with a cold, soggy mess.

Aerobic bacteria—the tiny, friendly, air-loving creatures that make compost cook—can't live in such an oxygen-poor environment. That kind of pile welcomes *anaerobic* bacteria, instead. These creatures will eventually make compost of your mess, but they work much more slowly than aerobic bacteria and the compost will be slimy and soggy during the 2 to 3 years it will take to decompose.

Actually, soggy compost is fairly easy to fix. If endlessly wet weather is part of the problem, cover the pile with a loose-fitting lid or tarp. You'll also need to turn the pile and fluff it up thoroughly. If you have some nitrogen-rich ingredients (such as fresh manure or shellfish wastes) and fibrous, nonmatting materials (such as shredded corncobs or sawdust), add them to help get things cooking.

---

quick tip

Use the following checklist to gauge the success of your finished compost:

Structure: Should be loose and crumbly—not too tight (like soil) and not lumpy

Color: Should be black-brown—not pure black or grayish yellow (signs of excess water)

Odor: Should be earthy-sweet—not bad-smelling (a sign that decomposition hasn't finished) and not musty (indicates the presence of molds)

pH: Should be neutral to slightly acidic

Moisture: Should be as moist as a damp sponge

Dry, Dusty Compost

This opposite version of soggy, slimy compost is extremely common from May through October in areas that receive little summer rainfall. No matter what materials you pile up, the stack just doesn't get enough moisture to support the bacterial life necessary to fuel the composting process. Luckily, curing dry, dusty compost is as simple as turning on a spigot. That's right—water your compost pile until the materials feel about as wet as a damp sponge.

Put an oscillating sprinkler on top of your dry compost pile and run it for about an hour. This will moisturize the materials better than running an open hose on top—especially if the outer layers are made up of materials such as straw or grass clippings, which tend to shed water when they dry out. After sprinkling, check the center of the pile to make sure it's moist. To moisten the entire pile, you might need to turn it and water the layers as you go.

If your compost is dry, put an oscillating sprinkler on top of the pile and run it for about an hour.

Turning and watering your pile should spring it to life fairly quickly. If not, you might have other problems, such as a lack of nitrogen-rich materials. If that's the case, tear the whole thing apart, add some grass clippings, manure, or bloodmeal to get it going, and pile it up again. When the pile starts cooking, don't let it dry out again. As those tiny organisms multiply, they use up a lot of water. You might have to water your compost almost as often as you water your roses during a heat wave.

Pill bugs live on the decaying matter in your compost pile.

Bugs!

Pill bugs and sow bugs are small crustaceans (not insects) that live on decaying organic refuse. If you turn your pile and see thousands of tiny, gray "armadillos" with seven pairs of legs each, you've discovered a nest of the primitive creatures. (Pill bugs roll up into a ball when threatened and sow bugs don't—otherwise, there isn't much difference between the two.)

These bugs won't harm your compost. In fact, they're actually helping to break it down. But if you don't remove them from the finished mixture before you spread it on the garden, you might find them snipping off the emerging roots and leaves of your garden plants.

Ants and earwigs also invade compost piles. Like sow bugs and pill bugs, they are essentially harmless to the composting process. Their presence may indicate that the breakdown process has nearly finished. Or, if you still have lots of material that hasn't broken down, these insects can simply mean that your pile is on a slow track to decomposition.

To get these bugs out of unfinished compost, raise the pile's temperature to above 120°F. Turn the pile over and rebuild it, watering it as you go. If it contains lots of slow-to-decompose materials, such as leaves or straw, mix in a nitrogen source, such as bloodmeal, manure, or shellfish wastes. It should soon start heating and, when it does, the bugs will depart for a more comfortable place.

But what if your sow-buggy compost is already finished and you want to use it on the garden without endangering small plants? Do you have to start all over again? Not if you de-bug it first! To do so, spread the compost in a thin layer on a tarp in direct sunlight and leave it there to dry.

By the way, if the dominant creature in your compost pile is the earthworm, give yourself a pat on the back! This is a sure sign that your compost has fermented, has decomposed, and is ready to spread. Transfer such worm-laden richness gently to your garden—the soil-churning activity of these organic heroes is something to encourage and be thankful for.

Bad-Smelling Compost

If your pile emits the sharp, nose-twisting stench of ammonia, it contains too much nitrogen-rich material (raw manure containing lots of urine is one likely culprit). It could also be too wet to allow aerobic bacteria to thrive. If it just "smells rotten" and there are lots of flies hanging around it, you've most likely added too many kitchen scraps or canning wastes without chopping them first or mixing them in thoroughly. For both cases, you should remake the pile to bring your stinky compost under control.

If too much "liquid nitrogen" is the problem, turn the pile and add absorbent materials—such as straw,

Compost should have an earthy smell; if your pile stinks, all is not well.

shredded tree leaves, or sawdust—as you go. Rebuild the pile to a height of 3 feet to get it cooking again.

If kitchen scraps, canning waste, or large amounts of other mucky stuff are producing offensive odors, you can turn the pile without adding anything. As you turn, break up all that mucky stuff and mix it in well. Remind yourself that you'll avoid this unpleasant task in the future by first finely chopping these materials and then by mixing them thoroughly into the heap.

Overheating

In cold weather, an active compost pile will emit steam, causing many beginning composters to think their pile is burning. What it's really doing, though, is "breathing" its warmth into the frosty air.

But if your compost is too nitrogen-heavy, the center *can* overheat and dry out, leaving visible white streaks. These white streaks are actually the dead bodies of millions of microorganisms. And, if they

Don't worry if your pile emits steam in cold weather. It's not burning—it's "breathing" its warmth into the frosty air.

hadn't been cooked, they would have been busy turning your pile into finished compost!

Sometimes called "fire fanging" or "burning" by old-time gardeners, this phenomenon is quite common in piles that have been overloaded with fresh manure (especially from chickens or horses). Regular turning and watering will help you keep such a nitrogen-rich pile under control. To correct an already fire-fanged pile, rebuild it completely, adding some slow-working, absorbent material, such as shredded corncobs or sawdust. Sprinkle the new materials with water as you add them.

Raccoons, Opossums, and Other Critters

If you spot raccoons, opossums, dogs, skunks, rats, or bears at your compost pile, they're probably going after the fresh, edible kitchen scraps you recently buried.

To avoid attracting animals, remember to keep meat scraps and fat out of your pile. Mix other kitchen scraps with soil and/or wood ashes, then bury them deeply into the hot center of the pile.

If animal scavengers have grown accustomed to getting a free meal from your compost pile,

Bury kitchen scraps deeply in the center of the pile to avoid tempting critters with a free meal.

you could have trouble breaking them of the habit. And unfortunately, this is one problem that can't be solved simply by turning or rebuilding the pile. You'll probably have to build or buy a covered container for your compost. (See "Tools and Supplies" on page 13 for more information on compost bins and containers.)

Plants Growing in the Pile

Transplant vegetable plants that have sprouted in your pile—or pull them out and add them to your next pile.

Young plants can emerge from a pile of finished, or nearly finished, compost. Invariably, a few seeds will survive the composting process (even a hot pile doesn't always heat up enough to kill all seeds). And the temperature, moisture, and fertility of the maturing compost are just about perfect for seed germination and seedling growth.

If the sprouts are weeds, just pull them out and add them to your next compost pile. (Green plants of any kind will provide nitrogen.) But if the young plants are vegetable or flower seedlings, go ahead and transplant them. Just be aware that they may be the offspring of hybrid parents and could, therefore, grow up to be something other than what you grew last season.

To avoid sprouts in future compost piles, don't add anything that contains seeds.

I Can't Turn My Compost Pile!

Most garden experts will tell you that a hot compost pile should be turned at least twice a month and as often as twice a week to keep it cooking.

But that turning can be difficult work. Seniors, disabled gardeners, and those who can garden only on weekends may be unable to do this.

If you can't turn your compost pile, relax—you can create this valuable soil amendment without turning. After all, nature doesn't need your help to decompose organic materials. And, if you build your cold pile correctly from the start, you'll avoid problems, such as bugs and unpleasant smells. Here's how.

Ensure complete breakdown of the materials that go into the pile by shredding and mixing them *before* piling them up. Put everything through a chipper/shredder, run a lawn mower over it, or use a pruning shears to cut up any large, coarse stems and stalks.

If that isn't possible, build the pile in layers—alternating "browns" (carbon-rich materials like leaves and straw) with "greens" (nitrogen-rich materials like grass clippings and kitchen scraps). Mix them together as you go.

Try to include some finished compost or rich topsoil in the mix to get things going, and water your pile as you build it. Keep the moisture level as even as possible. If the compost pile begins to dry out, water it with a sprinkler.

After 6 months to 1 year, you'll have finished compost—without ever turning the pile.

You can still make compost even if you can't turn your pile. Just build your pile in layers, alternating "browns" with "greens."

You can use compost in a variety of ways, including as a mulch or a side-dressing.

chapter five

Using Compost

Using compost is the key to having a healthy, beautiful, and productive garden. In this chapter, you'll find out how to know when compost is finished, when to use it, and how much to apply. Then you can just sit back and let this black gold work its magic in your soil.

FINAL RESULTS

For most garden uses, compost should be "well finished"—in other words, most of the organic materials in the pile have finished decomposing, leaving you with crumbly, dark humus. Unfinished compost can slow the germination and growth of many plants, so be especially careful to use finished compost in seed-starting mixes and seedbeds. (For fall applications or mulching, it's OK to use less-mature compost.)

WHEN IS IT FINISHED?

So how can you tell when you *do* have finished compost? Finished compost has a pleasant smell—earthy and sweet—and is a uniform dark brown color. Finished compost also is spongy, moist, and crumbly. If the pile had been hot, the temperature will have dropped and further turning won't cause it to heat up again. And other than the occasional corncob or eggshell, individual organic materials aren't identifiable.

For further proof that your compost is ready to use, try one of these two simple tests:

The sniff test. Put a handful of moist compost in a glass jar, seal the lid, then put the jar in a warm, sunny place. After 3 days, open the jar and sniff. Good-quality, finished compost should have an odor similar to that of freshly turned soil. If the compost smells rotten or foul, it isn't mature.

> **Finished compost smells earthy and sweet and is dark brown.**

EVEN FINISHED COMPOST sometimes contains large chunks of undecomposed or woody matter. For most garden uses, a few larger pieces here and there won't hurt. However, you should screen your compost before these uses.

- In potting mixes—larger pieces can block root growth inside pots

- On seedbeds—materials that haven't decomposed can inhibit germination or seedling growth

- For mulching perennial beds—where you want a more uniform look

- To eliminate unwanted bugs, such as sow bugs

You can either make your own compost screen or buy one. When screening compost, work over a wheelbarrow or garden cart, next to your compost pile. Wearing gloves, push the compost through the screen. Toss the large pieces into a new compost pile. Transport the screened compost wherever you need it.

The germination test. Mix together equal parts compost and potting soil. Plant lettuce or radish seeds in the mix. At the same time, plant the same kind and number of seeds in plain potting soil. If both groups of seeds germinate uniformly, the compost is safe to use. But if growth is slower in the compost mix, your compost isn't ready.

HOW TO USE IT

Finished compost is a versatile material that you can apply freely at any time of the year without fear of burning plants or polluting water. Here are just a few of the many ways you can use compost.

New Beds

Mix mature compost into new garden beds, 4 to 5 inches deep. The compost will improve the soil's fertility and texture, protect crops against disease and drought, buffer soil imbalances, and prevent erosion.

Annuals

Before you seed or transplant annual vegetables and flowers to garden beds, incorporate compost into the top inch or two of soil.

For a midsummer boost and disease protection, side-dress plants with compost—apply a thin layer on the soil next to the plants. Or, perk up plants by watering them with compost tea every couple of weeks. (To make compost tea, see "Brew Some Compost Tea" on page 67.)

To get a head start, you can work less-mature compost into the soil of vegetable beds in fall. By the following spring, when it's time to plant, the compost will have finished decomposing.

Perennials

Before planting long-lived perennials, work plenty of compost into the garden bed. After that, most perennials will appreciate an annual application of compost in early spring.

To apply, push back any mulch, then gently work the compost into the soil around the base of the plant. If the soil is dry, water after applying the compost, then replace the mulch.

Heavy feeders—such as astilbe, chrysanthemums, and peonies—benefit from a second application of compost mid-season, either by side-dressing or watering with compost tea.

Trees and Shrubs

When planting trees and shrubs, *don't* backfill the planting hole with compost-amended soil. This will only cause the roots to ball up inside the hole rather than branch out into the surrounding soil in search of much-needed nutrients. Instead, plant your tree or shrub first. Then, apply compost to the surface of the soil above the root zone.

Both annuals and perennials benefit from a boost of compost.

For moderate or heavy feeders, apply a layer of compost annually. (Remove mulch if you use it, then replace it after you apply the compost.) If your soil is poor, or the tree or shrub is growing too slowly, apply compost in both spring and fall.

Lawns

Spread compost when planting a new lawn. Also, apply compost at least once each season to rejuvenate an existing lawn. A ¼-inch layer is enough to feed the grass, prevent disease, and improve water retention.

Containers

Finished compost is excellent for use in containers—either as a seed-starting medium or in potting soils. Unlike common garden soil, compost contains few, if any, pathogens. On the contrary, compost contains *disease-suppressing* microbes.

Before you use compost in containers, screen it to remove large pieces. (Throw those pieces into your new compost pile.) Add sand, vermiculite, or other ingredients to create your own custom potting mix. *Reminder:* When starting seeds, use only *finished* compost.

Mulch

Spreading compost as a mulch suppresses weeds and conserves moisture as it simultaneously feeds nearby plants and protects them from disease. *Note:* To maximize compost's scientifically proven disease-preventing powers, use it *slightly before* it's fully matured and crumbly, and apply it as a surface mulch instead of digging it in.

Cover-Crop Decomposer

When turning under cover crops in late summer or fall, work a little compost into the soil at the same time.

STRAIGHT TO THE ROOTS

MANY ANNUALS benefit from a side-dressing of compost in midsummer. But if a spring rain comes along just after you've spread the compost, some of its benefits may run off into the garden path and away from your plants' root zone.

You can prevent that from happening by using a pointed hoe *before* you spread the compost. Drag the hoe beside the plants, about 4 inches from their centers, or far enough away so that you don't hill up soil on the plants' stems. Make a shallow trench along the row. Don't make the trenches deeper than 2 inches to avoid disturbing new roots.

Then, sprinkle your compost along the trench. The compost will do its work where you want it. When it rains, your plants will receive a drink of compost tea.

Finished compost will help the fresh green material decompose.

WHEN TO USE IT

If you plan to mix the compost into your garden soil as a fertilizer or amendment, the best time is 2 to 4 weeks before you begin planting. That'll give the compost enough time to stabilize in the soil. But if you plan to spread the compost on the surface of your soil as a disease-preventing mulch, you have two choices.

If you're growing lettuce, apply compost after the plants are up because fresh compost can inhibit the germination of lettuce seeds.

- You can either apply it several weeks before you plant

- Or apply it a few weeks after seeds have sprouted and the young plants are up and growing

That's because fresh compost can inhibit the germination of some seeds—particularly beans, radishes, lettuce, and some onions—especially in dry regions.

HOW MUCH TO USE

Sometimes, people get the idea that they need to bury their gardens with compost, but that isn't true. A surprisingly moderate layer will produce wonderful results. Here are some basic guidelines for how much compost to apply:

- For one-time applications to new garden beds, mix 1 to 2 inches of mature compost 4 to 5 inches deep into the soil. For new garden beds in the Deep South or high rainfall areas, double that initial, new-bed application to 2 to 4 inches.

- If you live in a very cold, short-season area (Zone 4 or colder), where the nutrients in compost aren't used up or leached away as fast, start with 1 inch for new beds, then add slightly less than ½ inch annually.

In midseason, side-dress heavy feeders such as corn with ¼ inch of compost.

quick tip

Do you have heavy, clay soil that doesn't dry out in time for you to plant early crops, such as spring peas or onions? If so, try making a "spring starting bed" using compost. Spread a 6-inch layer of compost over an area of untilled garden soil, forming a raised bed. Plant peas, lettuce, onions, or potatoes right in the compost. The raised compost bed will warm up fast and will contain just the right amount of moisture and nutrients to get plants off to a strong start.

- After the initial application, a yearly application of just ½ inch of compost that contains about 1 percent nitrogen will provide ample nutrients for excellent plant growth in most regions.

- If you garden in the South or in a region that has very high rainfall or sandy soil, double the annual rate to 1 inch.

- In midseason, side-dress heavy feeders (such as corn, tomatoes, and peppers) and fast-growers (such as cucumbers and squash) with ¼ inch of compost to keep plants growing strong.

- Before squeezing in a succession planting of vegetables, flowers, or cover crops, apply ⅛ to ¼ inch of compost (the higher amount in hot, sandy, or rainy areas) to get the planting off to a well-fed start.

Computing Compost Coverage

How do you know how much compost to spread to end up with a layer of a certain depth? Use these baseline measurements as a starting point:

- One 4 × 4-foot bin containing a 2-foot-high layer of finished compost = 32 cubic feet (or 237 gallons or 1,280 pounds). That's enough compost to cover 384 square feet with a 1-inch deep layer. (Generally, raw materials shrink to about half their original size as they decompose, so a 4-foot layer of materials becomes a 2-foot layer of finished compost.)

- One cubic yard of finished compost = 27 cubic feet (or 200 gallons or 1,080 pounds). That's enough compost to cover 324 square feet with a 1-inch layer.

- One 5-gallon bucket of finished compost = 1 cubic foot. It'll cover 8 square feet, 1 inch deep.

- To cover 100 square feet with a 1-inch layer, you'll need about 8.3 cubic feet of compost. If you "slice" one cubic foot of compost—12 × 12 × 12 inches—into 1-inch layers, it'll cover 12 square feet. So, dividing 100 square feet of beds by 12 square feet from each cubic foot of compost gives you 8.3 cubic feet.

Here's how to figure your compost needs:

1. Measure the area you want to cover with compost and determine the square footage.

2. Divide by 100.

3. Multiply by the thickness of the layer you want to spread.

4. Multiply that number by 8.3. This will tell you how many cubic feet of compost you need. (Keep in mind that a typical 4 × 4-foot bin holds 32 cubic feet of finished compost.)

One 4 × 4-foot bin containing a 2-foot-high layer of finished compost is enough to cover 384 square feet.

A handy "measuring cup" for finished compost is a 30-gallon garbage can. It holds about 4 cubic feet of finished compost. You also can measure the volume of your wheelbarrow or garden cart and use it as your measuring device.

HOW TO APPLY IT

To improve fertility and soil structure in new beds, mix the compost in as deep as you can. If you're double-digging your soil (loosening it at a deeper level than usual) or if you're planning to plant your crops close together for an intensive garden—

techniques that encourage plant roots to grow deeper than usual—you'll also want to mix your annual booster doses of compost into the soil.

Dug-in compost feeds your plants and improves the soil. As bacteria feed on compost, they produce carbohydrates (sugars and starches) that "glue" the soil's tiniest particles together into larger pieces called "aggregates." The more aggregates there are, the more porous the soil becomes, allowing vital air and water to easily reach plant roots. Fungi also feed on the elements in your compost. And as they do, their long thread like structures (called "hyphae") spread throughout the soil, "sewing" together the smaller aggregates. One group of fungi, the mycorrhizae, extends the reach of plant roots, allowing the plant to obtain water and nutrients hidden deep beneath the soil's surface.

But when your aim is to use compost to fight plant diseases, leave your compost on the surface of the soil. Extensive international research shows that compost has the power to prevent many common plant diseases as it feeds crops.

To get the maximum amount of disease-fighting power, mulch the surface of garden beds with *slightly immature* compost, if you have it. Areas that stand to benefit the most from surface applications of compost include:

- Gardens in the South, where plant diseases tend to be more common and severe
- Small vegetable gardens, where crop rotation is difficult from year to year
- Rose beds, where various diseases can build up
- Around fruit trees (compost has been shown to eliminate brown rot, a fungal disease of peaches and other stone fruits)
- On strawberry beds, where diseases are likely to build up

quick tip

After you've been composting for a year, you can celebrate by sharing your experiences with the readers of *Organic Gardening* magazine in its "Compost Corner" section. Send a description and photo of your compost pile to Compost Pin, *OG*, 33 E. Minor Street, Emmaus, PA 18098. You'll receive their nifty compost pin award in return.

MAKE YOUR OWN COMPOST SPREADER

Compost can be difficult to spread evenly because it's heavy when damp. That's especially true if you use it before it's fully decomposed (as for a disease-fighting mulch). So why not borrow an idea from farmers? Use a spreader. With a little ingenuity—and an old wheelbarrow—you can build a garden-size spreader that'll help you apply an even layer of compost to your garden.

How to Make It

Find an old wheelbarrow. Perhaps you already own one. If not, you probably can find one at a garage sale.

1. Using a saw with a metal cutting blade, carefully cut a "window" at the end of the wheelbarrow. Make the cuts right where the sides meet the bottom of the wheelbarrow. The opening should be 2⅓ to 3 inches wide and run from side to side at the front end of the wheelbarrow (the end over the wheel and opposite the handles).

2. Carefully bend the cut edges toward the outside of the wheelbarrow so you don't cut yourself on them when you use the compost spreader.

How to Use It

This tool works best if you pull the wheelbarrow behind you, rather than push it. Shake it from side to side as you go. The opening should be wide enough to drop clumps of compost as you pull it along.

You can turn an old wheelbarrow into a compost spreader in no time flat.

If you run out of homemade compost, you can always buy commercial compost to use on your beds.

chapter six

Commercial Compost

Homemade compost is the best thing you can use to feed your plants and improve your soil. But even if you make your own, there may be times when you don't have enough of it to go around. That's when commercial compost comes in handy.

PRODUCT INEQUALITY

Your local municipal compost site or garden center is certainly an option when it comes to loading up with bulk or bagged compost. But before you do, be forewarned: Not all commercial compost is created equal. Commercial composts are highly variable in organic matter and nutrient content. Some can even harm your soil and plants. Here's how to tell the difference between safe-to-use commercial composts and the stuff you should pass on.

> **Not all commercial composts are created equal.**

MUNICIPAL COMPOST

With landfill space decreasing and waste disposal costs rising, more communities are becoming involved in large-scale composting. In 1990, more than 1,000 municipal composting sites were operating in the United States. And new legislative limits on waste disposal and public demand for environmentally safe waste handling are sure to lead to more of these operations.

Municipal compost operations range from small leaf-composting facilities to huge systems capable of turning 800 tons of waste per day into compost. Most use mechanized turners and forced-air methods to break down the large volume of materials as fast as possible. A few are fully enclosed, automated "in-vessel" systems that take in refuse at one end and

A municipal site is a great place to find inexpensive compost.

sort, grind, mix, moisten, and aerate the material as it proceeds to the other end, where it emerges as finished compost.

Many municipal compost sites offer their product to local residents at little or no cost. Even if you must pay a small fee (common if you're not a resident), you'll still probably save compared to the cost of bagged compost, which sometimes reflects the cost of transportation.

To locate a municipal composting site near you, check township or city government listings in your phone book. Contact the office that manages solid waste. Most states also maintain a list of operating or planned compost facilities.

(Just remember that when you visit a municipal compost site, the compost won't be bagged—meaning you'll need containers or a pick-up truck in which to haul it.)

Using Municipal Compost

Because the quality of compost from municipal operations can vary considerably, you should keep the following tips for using municipal compost in mind.

- Never use municipal sludge or compost that contains sludge. Sludge (sometimes called "biosolids") may contain toxic heavy metals, such as cadmium, nickel, and copper, which can build up in soil.

- Use municipal compost on ornamental beds—not for edible plants. Municipal compost is made from yard wastes. And some of that plant debris probably was treated with herbicides, fungicides, or pesticides.

- Gauge the quality of the compost before you load up. Some piles will be more finished than others. Choose compost that has a uniform dark brown color and sweet, earthy odor—no hint of ammonia or sourness. It shouldn't contain visible wood chips, pine needles, or other materials that still need to decompose.

MUSHROOM COMPOST

If you live near a commercial mushroom grower, you may be able to buy mushroom compost—the medium used to grow mushrooms. Mushroom compost (also called "mushroom soil") is a blend of one-third horse manure, one-third spoiled hay, and one-third ground corncobs. With a 1.4–1–1 NPK value and a near-neutral pH, mushroom compost makes an excellent soil amendment.

A bulk load of mushroom compost (about 16 tons) costs about

Mushroom compost—a mixture of hay, corncobs, and horse manure—is a wonderful soil amendment.

NOT YOUR BACKYARD COMPOST

HOMEMADE COMPOST differs from commercial compost products in several key ways:

- Commercial compost piles are larger (commonly 8 feet tall and 16 feet wide, versus the 4 × 4-foot backyard compost pile). The size of commercial compost piles makes them difficult to mix and maintain, resulting in inconsistent quality.

- Many commercial composts are based around a single material, such as manure. (Homemade compost usually contains a mix of garden wastes, grass clippings, kitchen scraps, and leaves.) A single ingredient typically doesn't compost as well as a mix of materials. Commercial-compost makers don't always add other materials because of the extra time and cost involved.

Experts predict that we'll see more dry or dehydrated manure products marketed as compost. Many of these products claim to be fully composted, but aren't. And if you apply them at the same rate as other composts, they could burn plants because of their higher nitrogen content. If the label tells you that the product contains dehydrated manure, use it at a lower rate than mature compost.

$100—delivered. (Most places will deliver or fill a pickup truck with mushroom soil for just $5 to $10.)

Make sure you get *organic* mushroom compost, however. Organic growers use steam to kill weed seeds and competing fungi and molds—other mushroom composts may be chemically treated. One supplier of organic mushroom compost is Hawk Valley Farm in Kempton, Pennsylvania.

Eastern Pennsylvania is the "mushroom capital of the world," but mushroom growers are scattered throughout other regions, too. Check with your local Cooperative Extension office for the names of nearby growers in your area.

BAGGED COMPOST

If you're willing to pay a bit more, you can purchase commercial compost by the bag at your local garden center or home-improvement store. But be aware: Buying compost isn't as simple as looking for the best brand. Most commercial composts are produced and sold locally—you won't find the same products in South Dakota and Tennessee—or even in Nashville and Memphis.

The quality of commercial composts varies because they are usually made from whatever local waste materials are available at that time. For example, one batch might be made with low-salt manure and the next with high-salt manure. That means that unless the producer monitors each batch carefully, a brand that tests at the top of the class one month could flunk the next time around.

Organic Gardening magazine and Woods End Research Laboratory in Mount Vernon, Maine, tested 30 brands of bagged compost and found the following product problems:

- **More than half of the brands tested were too old or diluted with soil,** resulting in a low organic-matter content. If the level of organic matter is too low, the compost won't improve the soil as well as a better-quality product would. (High-quality, finished compost contains 30 to 60 percent organic matter.)

- **Nearly half of the samples tested had a pH outside the preferred 6.5 to 7.5 pH range.** For optimum growth of most plants, you want a near-neutral soil pH. Nine of the samples tested too high (as alkaline as 8.3 pH), and four of them tested too low (as acidic as 4.5).

- **A quarter of the samples contained too much salt.** If compost production isn't managed properly, or if a large amount of chicken manure is used, salts can accumulate to a level high enough to injure plants—especially seedlings.

- **A quarter of the samples were sticky and wet.** These compost products would have been difficult, if not impossible, to spread.

quick tip

How much compost should you buy for your garden? To get good results, you might need less than you think. In most areas of the country, a ½-inch-thick layer each year is plenty.

Nitrogen is the main nutrient you need to give your plants. And in most regions, a yearly rate of just ½ inch of compost containing 1 percent nitrogen (about four 40-pound bags or 30 gallons per 100 square feet) will provide ample nutrients and organic matter for excellent plant growth. In the longer growing seasons of the South and in areas with very high rainfall, double that annual rate to 1 inch. And for one-time applications to new garden beds, you can double that rate if you're sure you have good-quality compost.

Buying Quality Compost

Fortunately, a simple look and smell are all you need to do to find a good-quality product. If possible, ask your garden center or supplier to let you take home a few samples before you buy. Put the samples through your own round of testing, using the following criteria.

- **The texture should be loose and granular,** with little or no recognizable bark or wood. If the compost isn't loose enough for you to spread and work it easily into your garden beds, don't buy it.

- **The color should be dark brown or black-brown.** Avoid products that are light in color. They probably contain too little organic matter and too much soil. It's easiest to tell the true product color if you let the compost sample dry out.

- **The compost should be moist, not dry or soggy.** In the soil, compost can hold up to 2½ times its weight in water. But in bagged products, excess water makes the compost difficult to spread. (Plus, you'll be paying for water, not compost.) Simply lifting a bag of compost will give you a good idea of its moisture content. If it feels like a big glob, the compost probably is too wet. If it feels loose, it's probably drier.

- **Mature compost has a pleasant, earthy smell.** If you find an earthy, woodsy odor, you've probably struck "black gold"—a mature, good-quality compost. Avoid composts with a strong or unpleasant smell, indicating immature compost that could damage plants. (*Note:* Some good-quality bagged composts have a slight musty or barnyard odor when first opened. That's because the plastic bags restrict the oxygen supply to the organisms that release the earthy odor. After a day or two, the compost should acquire that earthy aroma.)

quick tip

If you buy commercial compost, try to buy only as much as you plan to use in a season. Although compost doesn't have an "expiration date," as it ages it loses its food value. Find yourself with too much compost? Add a layer to your lawn to help feed the grass and improve water retention. Or, share some with your neighbors!

● **Mature compost contains 30 to 60 percent organic matter.** To test the organic-matter content of any compost (commercial or homemade), spread some out on a thin layer of newspaper and let it air-dry for about a week. Then measure exactly 1 cup of the dried compost and weigh it. If it weighs between 4 and 6 ounces, it contains the desired amount of organic matter. If it weighs less than 4 ounces, it's probably immature. If it weighs more than 6 ounces, it's probably old or diluted with soil—so you shouldn't use it.

Commercial compost sold in plastic bags should have an earthy aroma a day or so after the bag is opened.

Some stores won't allow you to sample or inspect before you buy. If you buy a bag and find that it's not up to these standards, take it back and ask for a refund or dump it onto your home pile to dilute and fully compost it.

Another option is to look for bulk compost, sold at some garden centers. You'll not only be able to see what you're buying but also save some money. Many bulk composts are cheaper than bagged products: 1 cubic yard of bulk compost (the equivalent of twenty-five 40-pound bags) usually costs less than $30, while the good-quality bagged composts sell for $2 to $4 per 40-pound bag. Another advantage of bulk compost is that the garden center might be willing to deliver it right to your garden. (If they don't deliver door-to-garden, use your pick-up truck—or a neighbor's—to pick up your compost.)

Your Seasonal Guide to Composting

NOW YOU KNOW the complete story about compost: how it helps your soil; the ingredients you need to make it; different methods you can use to build a pile; and how to apply it. So to help you along in your compost-making endeavors, we've put together this month-by-month calendar, which will guide you through what to do when. (Believe it or not, making compost is really a year-round project, as there's something compost-related to do January through December.)

JANUARY

Consider starting a **worm** composting bucket or **bin** indoors, using newspapers as bedding material and kitchen scraps for food. Order your redworms through a garden-supply catalog.

FEBRUARY

Plan your **composting strategy**. Decide whether you want to buy a commercial bin, build your own, or just have a free-form pile. Find a shady spot on your property to place or **build the bin** or to build your free-form pile. Look for nearby sources of raw materials, such as **pine needles** or seaweed (depending on where you live).

MARCH

Find a source for finished compost (just in case your needs are greater than your means). Many **counties** and **municipalities** compost leaves and yard wastes for residents' use.

APRIL

Clean out your perennial and vegetable beds, and **add** the **winter mulch** that hasn't decomposed to your compost pile. Get those spring weeds out before they set seed and put them in your pile as well. **Dig finished compost** into your vegetable beds before planting. And **sidedress** your **perennials** with whatever compost you have left. If you

have a worm bin, you can move it outside to a shady spot (but keep it covered).

MAY

With the garden in full swing, you should have plenty of raw materials (such as **spent plants**, vegetable scraps, and weeds) to add to your compost pile.

- Keep adding ingredients to your pile until it's 3 to 4 feet high, and **turn** the pile **frequently** to keep it cooking.

- When your pile gets to be a good size (a 3- to 4-foot square), **start another**.

- If heavy rains are predicted, **throw a tarp** over your compost so it doesn't get sopping wet.

- Convince your grass-bagging neighbors to call you after they mow (but **leave** your own **clippings** on the lawn to benefit the soil)—and add the clippings to your pile (as long as your neighbors don't treat their lawns with chemicals).

Winter

Spring

Summer

Fall

JUNE

If you started a compost pile back in March or April, you might have some finished compost by now.

- **Screen out** the large pieces that haven't decomposed and put them in your working pile.

- **Check the pH** of the finished compost.

- As for the unfinished stuff, turn, turn, turn.

- Also **take its temperature**. A hot (150° to 160°F) pile will be more likely to kill diseases and seeds. If it isn't as hot as you'd like it to be, **add high-nitrogen** materials, like grass clippings or vegetable peelings.

JULY

Keep your compost moist (but not wet) during the hot midsummer days. You can **trap rainwater** by making a shallow depression on top. If your pile gets very dry, rebuild it, giving each 6- to 8-inch layer a **good sprinkling**.

AUGUST

You know the routine. Build the pile; turn the pile. Keep it moist; keep it hot. **Renew the soil** between plantings by digging in finished compost. There's no such thing as too much compost.

Take photos of your compost pile and of the lush gardens that are reaping the benefits of your homemade compost. (See "December" for what to do with the photos.)

SEPTEMBER

Spread a thin layer of compost on your lawn to keep the soil alive and healthy. As you clean out your vegetable and perennial beds and **compost** the old **stalks and stems**, remember to dispose of diseased plants and weeds that have gone to seed elsewhere.

OCTOBER

Leaves are falling!
- First, run over them with your **lawn mower**. Then you can use them on your vegetable and perennial beds, pile them in your compost bin, or bag them to **mix with** next summer's high-nitrogen **greens**. One way or the other, use your leaves.

- It's also time to clean out your worm bin. **Remove** most of the finished compost and most of **the worms**. The compost (castings) makes a high-nitrogen soil additive.

- **Share extra worms** with your friends, then move your worm bin indoors for the winter.

NOVEMBER

Continue to compost your **kitchen scraps** by toting them out to your compost pile, or by feeding them to your worms if you have a worm bin.

DECEMBER

Send a description and a photo of your composting success to *Organic Gardening* magazine's "Compost Corner" at Compost Pin, OG, 33 E. Minor Street, Emmaus, PA 18098—they'll send you a nifty pin!

A Glossary of Composting Terms

Now that you know all about making compost, you'll want to brush up on the lingo that goes with it as well. Learning the lingo will come in handy when you're referring to this book or reading materials pertaining to composting and soil care.

Aeration. The exchange of air in the pore spaces of the soil with air in the atmosphere. Good aeration is necessary for healthy plant growth.

Aerobic. Describes organisms living or occurring only when oxygen is present.

Anaerobic. Describes organisms living or occurring when oxygen is absent.

C:N ratio. The proportion of bulky, dry, high-carbon materials to dense, moist, high-nitrogen materials. The ideal C:N ratio for stimulating compost organisms is 25:1 to 30:1; finished compost's C:N ratio is about 10:1.

Clay soil. Soil made up of very fine particles. Holds water and nutrients but does not drain well and can be hard to work. When dry, can become clumpy.

Cold pile. A compost pile that receives little or no turning, allowing some anaerobic decomposition to occur; composting continues at cooler temperatures over a longer period of time.

Compost. Decomposed and partially decomposed organic matter that's dark and crumbly. Used as an amendment, compost increases the water-holding capacity and drainage of the soil, and is an excellent nutrient source of microorganisms, which later release nutrients to your plants.

Decomposer. Organisms, usually soil bacteria, that derive nourishment by breaking down the remains or wastes of other living organisms into simple organic compounds.

Fertilizer. A natural or manufactured material added to the soil that supplies one or more of the major nutrients—nitrogen, phosphorus, and potassium—to growing plants.

First-level consumer. A living thing that acquires all of the nutrients it needs to survive from soil alone. Sow bugs, grasses, other plants, and trees are examples of first-level (or primary) consumers.

Hot pile. A compost pile that's turned or otherwise aerated frequently, creating high temperatures and finished compost in a relatively short time.

Humus. A dark-colored, stable form of organic matter that remains after most of the plant and animal residues in it have decomposed.

Loam. The best texture for soil to have; it contains a balance of fine clay, medium-sized silt, and coarse sand particles. Loam is easily tilled and retains moisture and nutrients effectively.

Micronutrient. A nutrient plants need in very small quantities. Micronutrients include copper, chlorine, zinc, iron, manganese, boron, and molybdenum.

Organic. Materials that are derived directly from plants or animals. Organic gardening uses plant and animal by-products to maintain soil and plant health, and doesn't rely on synthetically made fertilizers, herbicides, or pesticides.

Organic matter. An organic soil substance that contains valuable nutrients. Can include kitchen or garden wastes, insects, sawdust, or any number of other compostable organic materials.

PH. A measure of how acid or alkaline a substance is. The pH scale ranges from 1.0 to 14.0, with 7.0 indicating neutrality, below 7.0 acidity, and above 7.0 alkalinity. The pH of your soil has a great effect on which nutrients are available to your plants.

Sandy soil. Soil that contains more than 70 percent sand and less than 15 percent clay. Sandy soil is generally easy to work with and well drained, but it has few nutrients and poor water-holding ability.

Second-level consumer. A living thing that acquires all of the nutrients it needs to survive from first-level consumers. Mites, mice, and frogs are examples of second-level (or secondary) consumers.

Sheet composting. A method of spreading undecomposed organic materials over the soil's surface, then working them into the soil to decompose, rather than piling them and spreading the resulting compost.

Side-dress. To apply solid (as opposed to liquid) fertilizer alongside annual plants during the growing season.

Silt. Refers to a soil particle of moderate size—larger than clay but not as large as sand.

Soil amendment. A material added to the soil to make it more productive by improving its structure, drainage, or aeration. An amendment such as compost can also be used to enhance microbial activity.

Soil structure. The physical arrangement of soil particles and interconnected pore spaces. Soil structure can be improved by adding organic matter.

Soil test kit. A set of instructions and a soil bag available through your state's Cooperative Extension Service. Test results indicate soil pH and specify which amendments you should add to your soil.

Third-level consumer. A living thing that acquires all of the nutrients it needs to survive from second-level consumers. Eagles, owls, spiders, and beetles are examples of third-level (or tertiary) consumers.

Top-dress. To apply compost or fertilizer evenly over a bed of growing plants.

Recommended Reading & Resources

Books & Periodicals

Appelhof, Mary. *Worms Eat My Garbage.* Kalamazoo, MI: Flower Press, 1982.

Campbell, Stu. *Let It Rot: The Gardener's Guide to Composting.* Charlotte, VT: Storey Communications, 1975.

Gershuny, Grace. *Start with the Soil.* Emmaus, PA: Rodale, 1993.

Hynes, Erin. *Rodale's Successful Organic Gardening: Improving the Soil.* Emmaus, PA: Rodale, 1994.

Martin, Deborah, and Grace Gershuny, eds. *The Rodale Book of Composting.* Emmaus, PA: Rodale, 1992.

Ondra, Nancy J. *Soil and Composting: The Complete Guide to Building Healthy, Fertile Soil.* (Taylor's Weekend Gardening Guides.) Boston: Houghton Mifflin, 1998.

Organic Gardening magazine. Rodale, 33 E. Minor Street, Emmaus, PA 18098.

Rodale, Maria. *Maria Rodale's Organic Gardening.* Emmaus, PA: Rodale, 1998.

Stell, Elizabeth P. *Secrets to Great Soil.* Pownal, VT: Storey Communications, 1998.

Tools & Supplies

Bountiful Gardens
18001 Shafer Ranch Road
Willits, CA 95490-9626
Phone: (707) 459-6410
Fax: (707) 459-1925
Web site: www.bountifulgardens.org

Cape Cod Worm Farm
30 Center Avenue
Buzzards Bay, MA 02532
Phone: (508) 759-5664
Web site: members.aol.com/Capeworms/private/wormhome.htm

Gardener's Supply Co.
128 Intervale Road
Burlington, VT 05401-2850
Phone: (800) 863-1700
Fax: (800) 551-6712
Web site: www.gardeners.com

Happy D Worm Ranch Farm
P.O. Box 3001
Visalia, CA 93278
Phone: (559) 738-9301
Fax: (559) 733-3250
Web site: www.happydranch.com

Harmony Farm Supply and Nursery
3244 Gravenstein Highway North
Sebastopol, CA 95472
Phone: (707) 823-9125
Fax: (707) 823-1734
Web site: www.harmonyfarm.com

Johnny's Selected Seeds
1 Foss Hill Road
R.R. 1, Box 2580
Albion, ME 04910-9731
Phone: (207) 437-4301
Fax: (800) 437-4290
Web site: www.johnnyseeds.com

Lee Valley Tools, Ltd.
12 East River Street
Ogdensburg, NY 13669
or
1090 Morrison Drive
Ottawa, Ontario K2H 1C2
Phone: (800) 871-8158
Fax: (800) 513-7885
Web site: www.leevalley.com

Peaceful Valley Farm Supply
P.O. Box 2209
Grass Valley, CA 95945
Phone: (530) 272-4769
Fax: (530) 272-4794
Web site: www.groworganic.com

Plow & Hearth
P.O. Box 6000
Madison, VA 22727-1600
Phone: (800) 627-1712
Fax: (800) 843-2509
Web site: www.plowhearth.com

Seeds of Change
P.O. Box 15700
Santa Fe, NM 87506-5700
Phone: (888) 762-7333
Fax: (888) 329-4762
Web site: www.seedsofchange.com

Smith & Hawken
Two Arbor Lane, Box 6900
Florence, KY 41022-6900
Phone: (800) 940-1170
Fax: (606) 727-1166
Web site: www.smith-hawken.com

Acknowledgments

Contributors to this book include Mary Appelhof, Christine Bucks, Eliot Coleman, Matt Damsker, Carol Keogh, Cheryl Long, Scott Meyer, and Catherine Yronwode.

Photo Credits

AG Stock 40 (top)

Matthew Benson 66

Rob Cardillo 68 (all)

Walter Chandoha vi, 74, 83, 96–97

Bruce Coleman Photography 38

Bruce Coleman Photography/J. C. Carto 28

Bruce Coleman Photography/ Matt Bradley 62

Corbis 30, 50

Grace Davis 67

E. R. Degginger 40 (middle), 40 (bottom), 41 (middle), 41 (bottom)

Dembinsky Photo 42 (top), 42 (bottom), 43 (top), 43 (bottom)

Grant Heilman 3, 44 (top)

David Liebman 69

Mitch Mandel i, 5, 7, 12, 14, 15 (top), 15 (bottom), 16, 17, 18, 19, 20, 21 (all), 22 (all), 23, 34, 49, 60, 64, 71, 76, 77, 78, 81, 84, 85, 88, 90, 91

Alison Miksch 25, 46

PhotoDisc 58

Troy Schnyder 73

Susan Seubert iv

Ron Weight 75

Ron West 41 (top), 42 (middle), 44 (bottom), 72

Kurt Wilson 9, 10, 27, 32, 95

Location Credit

Rodale Institute Experimental Farm, Maxatawny, Pennsylvania i, 12, 14, 15 (both), 16, 17, 18, 19, 25, 27, 34, 46, 49, 64, 71, 77, 78, 81, 84, 85

Index

USDA Plant Hardiness Zone Map

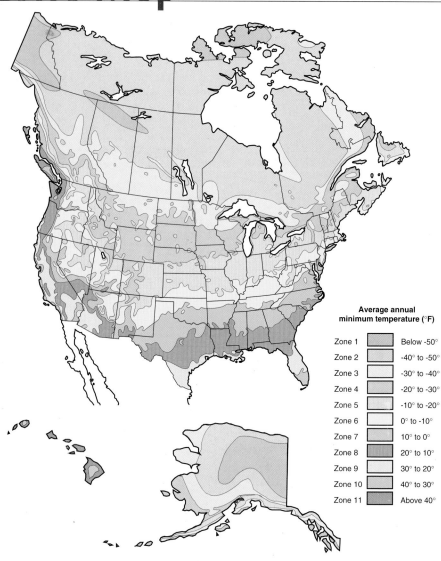

Average annual minimum temperature (°F)

Zone 1	Below -50°
Zone 2	-40° to -50°
Zone 3	-30° to -40°
Zone 4	-20° to -30°
Zone 5	-10° to -20°
Zone 6	0° to -10°
Zone 7	10° to 0°
Zone 8	20° to 10°
Zone 9	30° to 20°
Zone 10	40° to 30°
Zone 11	Above 40°

This map was revised in 1990 and is recognized as the best indicator of minimum temperatures available. Look at the map to find your area, then match its color to the key. When you've found your color, the key will tell you what hardiness zone you live in. Remember that the map is a general guide; your particular conditions may vary.